How Buffett Does It

24 Simple Investing Strategies from the World's Greatest Value Investor

James Pardoe

McGraw-Hill

New York   Chicago   San Francisco   Lisbon
London   Madrid   Mexico City   Milan   New Delhi
San Juan   Seoul   Singapore   Sydney   Toronto

9 0 DOC/DOC 0 9 8

ISBN 0-07-144912-4

McGraw-Hill books are available at special quantity discounts to use as premiums and sales promotions, or for use in corporate training programs. For more information, please write to the Director of Special Sales, Professional Publishing, McGraw-Hill, Two Penn Plaza, New York, NY 10121-2298. Or contact your local bookstore.

First Edition

How Buffett
Does It

John Lewis

'05

(07455-763-738)
John Lewis

Contents

How Buffett
Does It

☑ The Warren Buffett Way

For most of us, the stock market is a mystery. Given the abundance of choice—some 7,000+ stocks in the United States alone—how in the world do you make money investing in the stock market? Which stocks should you buy? Who should you listen to? What strategy should you follow?

Many of us are still recovering from the Internet stock crash and are still wary of putting our hard-earned money in the market. Many of us have learned the hard way. It might have been because of a friend's can't-miss stock tip, a stockbroker's recommendations, or a technology stock gone bust. One lesson learned by many is that get-rich-quick schemes all too often are get-poor-quick schemes.

If you are an investor who has been burned—whether by brokers, the Nasdaq crash, mutual funds, day trading, timing-the-market systems, penny stocks, options, or high-tech, high-growth companies—you really should study Warren Buffett's investment philosophy and approach.

A study of Warren Buffett reveals a proven *get-rich-slow* method for investing in the stock market. Buffett has turned acorns into oak trees through sound investment practices. You, too, can become a sound investor and make money in the stock market over the long term—but only if you follow his fundamental concepts and adopt his discipline, patience, and temperament.

Warren Buffett did not inherit one cent from his parents. Today, solely through his own investments, he is personally worth more than $40 billion. But from Harvard in the East to Stanford in the West, Buffett is rarely a topic of discussion in the classrooms of the top business schools. In other words, the greatest investor of all time is mostly ignored by academia.

I hope that *you* won't ignore Buffett's example. I hope that you will consider emulating his investment practices, especially if your previous investment experiences have been unpleasant.

In basketball, a mastery of the fundamentals is crucial to being a good player. A mastery of Buffett's investing fundamentals is crucial to being a sound value investor. These fundamentals include

1. A preference for simplicity over complexity

2. Patience

3. Proper temperament

4. Independent thinking

5. Ignoring distracting macro events

6. The counterintuitive strategy of nondiversification

7. Inactivity, not hyperactivity

8. Buying shares and then holding on to them for dear life

9. A focus on business results and value, not on the share price

10. Aggressive opportunism, seizing an opportunity when it is presented by stock market folly

These fundamentals, as well as others, will make you a better investor. Sound investment principles produce sound results.

Find a great business with great management, says Buffett, and buy shares at a sensible price—and then hold on to them for dear life.

CHAPTER 1

✔ **Choose Simplicity over Complexity**

When investing, keep it simple. Do what's easy and obvious, advises Buffett; don't try to develop complicated answers to complicated questions.

Many people believe that investing in the stock market is complex, mysterious, and risky and therefore is best left to the professional. This common mind-set holds that the average person can't be a successful investor because success in the stock market requires an advanced business degree, a mastery of complicated mathematical formulas, access to sophisticated market-timing computer programs, and a great deal of time to constantly monitor the market, charts, volume, economic trends, and so on.

Warren Buffett has shown this to be a myth.

Buffett has figured out a successful way to invest in the stock market that is not complex. Anyone with average intelligence is more than capable of being a successful value investor, without the assistance of a professional, because the fundamentals of sound investing are easy to understand.

Buffett will only invest in easy-to-understand, solid, enduring businesses that have a simple explanation for their success, and he never invests in anything complicated that he does not understand.

> **Remember that degree of difficulty does not count in investing. Look for long-lasting companies with predictable business models.**

The essence and beauty of Buffett's investment philosophy is its simplicity. It doesn't require complicated math, a financial background, or knowledge of how the economy or stock market will fare in the future. It is based on common-sense principles and patience—midwestern values that any investor can understand and implement. In fact, Buffett believes that investors do not help themselves when they rely on such things as mathematical formulas, short-term market forecasts or movements, or charts based on price and volume.

In fact, says Buffett, complexity can work *against* you. Don't drive yourself crazy trying to decode the latest theories about investing, such as options pricing or betas. In most cases, you're better off not even knowing about these cutting-edge systems. An important lesson that Buffett learned from his mentor, Ben Graham, was that you don't have to do "extraordinary things to get extraordinary results."

Keep it simple. Here's your goal: Buy stock in a great company, run by honest and capable people. Pay less for your share of that business than that share is actually worth in terms of its future earning potential. Then hold on to that stock and wait for the market to confirm your assessment.

This is the core principle of Buffett's philosophy of investing. It explains all his incredible achievements. It explains how he turned a $10.6 million *Washington Post* stock investment into a holding presently worth more than $1 billion, how he made a $1 billion Coca-Cola stock investment that today is worth more than $8 billion, and how he bought $45 million worth of GEICO Insurance shares and saw his investment grow to more than $1 billion.

> **If you don't understand a business, don't buy it.**

Buffett has turned Berkshire Hathaway into a $100 billion-plus company using this simple guiding principle. When investing in the stock market, he puts his money in easy-to-understand, solid businesses with strong, enduring prospects and capable and ethical management in place. He buys lots of shares when the stock market is selling them at a discount. In a nutshell, this explains his success.

Forget sophisticated stock-picking computer programs that key on price history, volatility, or market direction. Furthermore, discard equations full of logarithms and Greek letters. Buffett does use a computer—but mainly to play bridge and not to track stock price movements. Your investment goal should be the same as Buffett's: on the lookout for reasonably priced shares in understandable businesses that have a strong likelihood of higher earnings growth in the years to come. That's it!

Here are three principles that should underlie *all* your investment decisions:

Always keep it simple. Don't make investing unnecessarily hard. Stick with what you know and buy solid businesses that have strong and ethical management. Investment decisions that involve complexity should be avoided.

Make your own investment decisions. Be your own investment advisor. Beware of brokers and other salespeople who aggressively push an individual stock or mutual fund to fatten their commissions. Obviously, these individuals don't have your best interest at heart.

Study the man who Buffett studied under. The man who had the greatest influence on Buffett besides his father, Howard, was Benjamin Graham, the father of value investing, who taught Buffett decades ago that success in investments doesn't necessarily grow out of complexity. It's a good idea to read what he has to say.

Don't forget that Buffett's simple strategies have led to his extraordinary results.

CHAPTER 2

✔ Make Your Own Investment Decisions

Don't listen to the brokers, the analysts, or the pundits. *Figure it out for yourself.*

Warren Buffett believes that the average person is capable of investing successfully without relying on brokers, stock market pundits, or any other professional. And Buffett goes a big step farther. By and large, he says that these so-called experts *bring nothing* to the party. Whatever they claim to do, you can do better for yourself.

For obvious reasons, professional investors want you to think otherwise. They foster the belief that stock market investing is too complicated for the average person because that's good for *their* business. How long would they last if the average investor decided that they bring nothing to the party?

Maybe you have a hard time believing that all these experts whom you see on TV and hear on the radio don't actually add value. If so, you should consider how these professionals earn their income and what financial incentives govern their behavior. Financial professionals frequently are salespeople peddling investment products from which they derive financial benefit. A broker's income often is based on activity—commissions made through the buying and selling of shares.

Logically, then, brokers usually don't earn income when their clients hold stocks long term, which is a central tenet of Buffett's philosophy. *Activity* is often a broker's foremost concern. Brokers get paid based on the number of trades an investor makes, regardless of whether the investments are wise moves or ill-advised.

> **When approached by an investment advisor or other financial expert, ask, "What's in it for them?" If their answer is not satisfactory, walk away.**

By embracing Buffett's simple and proven ideas, you can dispense with the professional services of brokers, Wall Street pundits, computer stock-picking programs, market forecasters, and other self-appointed experts. You can make your *own* investment decisions. The people in most professions, Buffett acknowledges, add value beyond what the layperson can hope to achieve. Not so, he says, collectively in the field of money management.

Why? Well, most professionals ignore Buffett's basic philosophy and instead use complex investment practices of dubious utility. This, too, is understandable. Many of these financial professionals have had sustained (and expensive) educations, which have provided them with all sorts of exotic tools and techniques. As the old saying goes, give a kid a hammer and everything starts to look like a nail.

To be fair, most financial professionals certainly *believe* in their particular formulas and practices, which they have worked long and hard to master. Unfortunately, many of these professionals continue to ignore the practice of *value investing*, the technique pioneered a half-century ago by Benjamin Graham and Dave Dodd in *Security Analysis* and endorsed for almost four decades by Warren Buffett. Value investing consists chiefly of acting on discrepancies between price and value in the stock market: the figurative search for dollar bills that are selling for 40 cents.

> **Become a value investor. It's proven to be a very rewarding technique over the long term.**

Like Buffett, you can make money through value investing. The financial professionals whom you will be ignoring will *not* make money—at least on your account. Maybe that's why, despite Buffett's highly visible successes, there's been no apparent stampede toward embracing value investing. There are too many vested interests pushing in the opposite direction.

My argument—which grows out of Buffett's model—is that you should embrace value investing. You should be confident that Buffett's "commandments" are all you need to be self-reliant. They provide a framework that will enable you to take control of your financial future. For starters, try following these basic tenets of Buffett's method:

Gain some basic knowledge of accounting and the financial markets. To make your own investment decisions, you will need to learn about the basics of accounting and businesses in the stock market. Start reading financial periodicals and magazines—and, of course, everything you can on Benjamin Graham, Warren Buffett, and Charlie Munger.

Approach financial advisors, brokers, and "talking head" prophets with a healthy dose of skepticism. Once you acquire the fundamentals of investing, make sure that you are not "taken in" by financial "experts." Remember that most have vested interests or agendas that don't necessarily put your financial well-being first.

Remember that no one has a better investment record than Buffett. When trying to make sense of the stock market, it's a good idea to listen to the person making the most "cents."

An understanding of Buffett's ideas and practices will provide you with a code of conduct that you can follow yourself without needing the services of anyone else.

CHAPTER 3

☑ **Maintain Proper Temperament**

Let other people overreact to the market, Buffett advises. Keep your head when others do not, and you will benefit.

Although it is simple and easy to understand, Warren Buffett's investment philosophy is not necessarily easy to practice. Once you have armed yourself with an understanding of Buffett's approach, the next most important thing to develop is the proper temperament for a sound investor. Proper temperament means keeping your head at all times.

It means having the right state of mind when you have to deal with the inevitable bad news and setbacks that affect your stock holdings. Steeliness and poise are required when things go south. But proper temperament also means keeping your head at the other extreme: when the stock market is soaring, and people all around you are being greedy and euphoric.

Your temperament will come into play when things do not go your way. What will you do when confronted with a precipitous drop of a stock you own? Will you panic and sell your shares? What will you do in the face of a significant political or macroeconomic event such as a war, a recession, or a big decline in the Dow Jones average?

What will you do if the company you have stock in has an inevitable bad quarter or year? Are you going to be fixated on the daily price of the share or instead focus on long-term business fundamentals and results? What will be your reaction when a Wall Street expert predicts doom and gloom for your stock or for the stock market in general?

What will you do when the investment community is in the midst of a bear or bull market, permeated with either "speculative enthusiasm or depression" and gripped by either fear or euphoric greed, as was the case during the Internet bubble? Ben Graham, Buffett's professor at Columbia, once said, "The investor's chief problem, even his worst enemy, is likely to be himself." Will you be your own worst enemy?

Your reaction and response to these developments will play a tremendous role in determining your investment success. The wise investor remains calm in the face of negative events. Will you dump your shares when the price falls, or will you instead look to take advantage of a potential opportunity and buy more shares when they go "on sale"?

Buffett has a clear yardstick that you should apply to yourself. If you're someone who is likely to come unglued when one of your holdings loses half its value overnight, you shouldn't be in the stock market in the first place. You need to have the skill to invest in fine companies—and then the confidence to stick with them when others do not. It almost never makes sense to sell a good company, says Buffett, when there's fear in the air.

> **Don't own any stock that would cause you to panic and dump your shares if the price falls by 50 percent.**

Berkshire Hathaway experienced its worst year ever in 1999, while the Nasdaq was reaching new highs during the Internet frenzy of the late 1990s. Buffett's "outmoded" style of patient investing in low-tech companies was deemed obsolete. His refusal to buy hot high-tech stocks made him irrelevant—or so said the experts. Value investing was a dinosaur, and day trading was all the rage.

Consequently, in March 2000, the price of Berkshire Hathaway A shares fell by 50 percent to $40,000 a share from a previous high of $84,000 a share. Although the underlying business was still solid and its future secure, nervous shareholders dumped their Berkshire Hathaway shares. They were acting on *emotion* as a storm was battering Berkshire Hathaway, and they jumped off the ship instead of tethering themselves to it more tightly.

What does the Buffett approach mean? It means seeing a 50 percent drop in share price as a buying opportunity. It means keeping your eye on the fundamentals of the businesses in which you're invested rather than on the swings of a fickle market. If investors had heeded this advice and purchased Berkshire when its stock price dropped by 50 percent, they would have been richly rewarded when the stock price rebounded in 2004, skyrocketing to $97,000 a share.

Yes, it's all too easy to lose your cool in the midst of a hot stock market. It's even harder to stay calm when prices are plummeting and experts and magazine covers promise doom and gloom. In fact, the easiest thing to do in the latter case is to panic. *Don't.* When you own stock in a great business, keep it. If someone wants to sell you more at a bargain-basement price, buy it.

When Buffett was about 22 years old, he had accumulated about 350 shares of GEICO Insurance that were worth about $15,000; he then decided to sell all those shares. It turns out that if he had held on to those shares, they would have been worth about $1.3 million 20 years later. Through this experience and others, Buffett learned the hard way about selling his piece of a company that he had already identified as a wonderful business. He later remedied his mistake by buying major positions in GEICO in 1976—and by buying the entire company in 1996.

Here are three pieces of advice that will help you during good times and bad:

Hold on to great businesses. Do not be taken in by the stampede mentality (whether toward or away from the market). Buy great companies and hold them for years. Do not dart in and out of stocks. Research shows that the more investing one does, the more money one is likely to lose—plus, there are all those extra commissions you'll be paying.

Know yourself. Don't buy a stock if you cannot stomach it losing half its value. This means having the patience and discipline to hold on to companies with sound management and fundamentals.

Never make an investment decision because others tell you to. Develop a tin ear to hot stock tips, "talking heads," and others who may have a vested interest in a certain stock position. Do your homework and think for yourself.

To succeed in the market, says Buffett, you need only ordinary intelligence. But in addition, you need the kind of temperament that can help you ride out the storms and stick to your long-term plans. If you can stay cool while those around you are panicking, you can prevail.

CHAPTER 4

☑ Be Patient

Think 10 years, rather than 10 minutes, advises Buffett. If you aren't prepared to hold a given stock for a decade, don't buy it in the first place.

When Warren Buffett was 11 years old, he made his first stock purchase: three shares of Cities Service Preferred at $38 a share. Shortly thereafter, he sold his three shares when the price hit $40, earning him a net profit of $5. A few years later, this same stock was selling for $200 a share. Buffett learned early on about the need for *patience in investing*.

Buffett is a "decades trader" rather than a day trader. Buffett's philosophy is based on patience and a long-term outlook. It is a proven get-rich-slow scheme.

Day traders (or "swing traders") like to dump shares after weeks or even days. Buffett holds on to shares for years or even decades. Buffett has described the stock market as a "relocation center"—a means whereby money moves from the impatient to the patient. Which strategy makes more sense? Well, think about it: How many day traders have ever turned $10 million into $1 billion?

> **Learn to practice Buffett's discipline of patience. It will help you to amass greater stock market profits in the long term.**

It's worth remembering that some markets are actually hostile to in-and-outers, whereas they are friendly to buy-and-holders. In the 1970s and 1980s, Buffett has observed, company valuations were low, and stock prices didn't move all that quickly. People who jumped around wasted a lot of time and money—and then missed out on the big upsurge of the 1990s. Most people don't talk about the market opportunities they've blown. To his credit, Buffett does. And the moral of his stories is usually *buy and hold*. Patience is required for successful value investing. Impatience cost Buffett dearly when he bought a significant number of Disney shares for 31 cents a share in 1966 and then sold out the next year at 48 cents a share.

Charlie Munger, Buffett's long-time business partner, shares Buffett's view on the need for patience but expresses it more succinctly: "Investing is where you find a few great companies and then sit on your ass." He adds: "It's a mistake in investing to be too fretful. Patience is part of the game."

Here's a mental exercise that Buffett recommends. Imagine, when you buy a stock, that the markets closed the next day for a five-year holiday. Buffett says that he wouldn't think twice about such a turn of events because he almost never buys a stock with the intent to "flip" it. Buffett sets out to make money on a company rather than on the stock market. The market is simply the intermediary in your value-adding proposition. Think about other self-imposed disciplines that might help you maintain a patient outlook.

No, it is not easy being patient, but it is an absolutely critical component of having the proper temperament in value investing. When you invest, consider yourself as a permanent resident and not as a transient. A French city planner was once cautioned that he should not plant shade trees along the broad boulevards of Paris because they wouldn't mature for 80 years. His response? *"My god, man, then we'd better plant them right away!"* Buffett makes the same point when he observes that we can sit in the shade today because someone planted a tree many years ago.

It takes *time* for an acorn to grow into an oak tree. There are at least 25 families in Omaha, Nebraska, who have held on to their Berkshire shares for over 35 years, and their holdings are now worth over $100 million. Their original investments were $50,000 at most.

Buffett swims against the transient tide both as an investor and as the head of a major corporation. When it comes to the owners of Berkshire Hathaway, Buffett says that he wants people who have a personal commitment to the company. Don't regard your ownership position as simply a piece of paper whose value bounces around minute to minute (even though it *does* bounce). Instead, he advises, think of your stake as you'd think of a piece of real estate that you purchased in common with other members of your family. Would you sell the family farm or the family apartment building in response to some relatively minor external disruption? Of course not. Well, says Buffett, think of your equities the same way.

Buffett has owned a large block of Berkshire Hathaway shares for over 40 years. He has never sold a single share. He has lived through all the dramatic market swings, from Black Monday to the Dow breaking the 11,000-point psychological barrier, and he has never lost his head. It's not a simple contrarian viewpoint—that is, buy when others are selling and sell when others are buying. Instead, it's a commitment to keeping a cool head. Don't get swept up in others' "irrational exuberance" (as Alan Greenspan once famously phrased it). And don't succumb to the Chicken Little mentality. If you're taking the long view, the sky is *not* falling.

Ben Graham observed in *The Intelligent Investor*—Buffett's favorite investment book—that "we have seen much more money made and kept by 'ordinary people' who were temperamentally well suited for the investment process than by those who lacked this quality, even though they had an extensive knowledge of finance, accounting, and stock market lore."

In other words, it's all about understanding the big picture rather than being steeped in the technical details. One reason Buffett was able to turn a $10 million *Washington Post* investment into a *$1 billion* stake is that he has held on to those shares for dear life. Right after his purchase in 1973, the *Washington Post* share price dropped 50 percent, and the stock slumped for two years. Buffett did not sell a single share. He kept the big picture in mind.

Over the following years, the *Washington Post* faced great adversity, ranging from a labor strike to its role in Watergate, recessions, war, and the stock market crash of October 19, 1987—Black Monday—when the Dow fell 508 points.

Buffett still declined to sell any shares during these difficult times because he kept the big picture in mind. His patience has been richly rewarded: He makes his original investment back *every* year with an annual *Washington Post* dividend check of $10 million.

To Buffett, it was a volatile *stock* but not a volatile *business*. There is a profound difference between the two. There might have been fluctuations in the share price because of market chaos, but the underlying business was strong and secure. He never panicked. He held on, and the results speak for themselves.

The same applies for those Berkshire shareholders who have held on to their shares through thick and thin. The price of a Berkshire Hathaway A share was $40 in 1974, $1,275 in 1984, $15,400 in 1994, and $97,000 in 2004. Those investors with the proper temperament have been rewarded, whereas those who sold their shares are sorry.

Many things—good and bad—are going to happen while you are a shareholder. In other words, expect a sleigh ride. The stock market will overheat, and prices will skyrocket. The bears will close in, and prices will plunge. Again, the important thing is to *be in the right businesses and cultivate the right attitude*.

> **Don't dwell on the price of stocks. Instead, study the underlying business, its earnings capacity, its future, and so on.**

Here are a few tips straight from the Berkshire Hathaway playbook:

Heed Charlie Munger's advice. Sit on your ass. Do not mistake activity for achievement. When it comes to investing, the opposite is true.

Buy only stocks that you won't trade for five years or more. When you buy a stock, pretend that the stock market will be closed for the next five years and you cannot sell the stock, forcing you to adopt a long-term outlook.

Remember that "time is the friend of the wonderful business." Do not check your investments every day or week; remember that all stocks go up and down. A better use of your time would be to keep an eye on business performance rather than on price performance.

If the question is, "How long will you wait?"— in other words, how long will you hold a particular stock—Buffett's answer is, *"If we're in the right place, we'll wait indefinitely."*

CHAPTER 5

☑ BUY BUSINESSES, NOT STOCKS

Once you get into the *right business*, you can let everyone else worry about the stock market.

According to Warren Buffett, one critical factor in successful investing is to remember that you are buying *part of an actual business*. The stock is nothing in and of itself; instead, it's a representation of a real enterprise. When you think about your portfolio, what should come to mind is not Bloombergs, tickers, or tables of small type in the *Wall Street Journal*. What should come to mind, says Buffett, is a business or a collection of businesses— real enterprises engaged in the right businesses.

In other words, it's not about "playing the market"; it's about buying businesses—the *right* businesses. In the long run, the right business almost can't *help* but prosper. By the same token, the wrong business simply can't deliver the goods—short term *or* long term.

The most important thing that you can do before buying a stock, then, is to think long and hard about the underlying business and its future and view yourself not simply as an investor but as a business analyst. Pay attention to the price, of course—but pay more attention to value. ("Price" and "value" ought to be closely connected, of course, but in many cases they get disconnected.) Value grows out of what the business is doing, how well it is doing it compared to the competition, the scale on which it is doing it, and how those factors project into the future. The smart investor is the one who picks a "valuable" business based on these kinds of assessments.

When it comes to investing, Buffett emphasizes, it's all about the *performance* of the business behind the investment. What is the business doing, and how well is it doing it (in both a relative and absolute sense)? Investing is never emotional; it is always what Buffett calls "business-like."

Business performance **is the key to picking stocks. Study the long-term track record of any company that is on your buy list.**

In 1985, Buffett analyzed the largest U.S. textile company and its business results from 1964 to 1985. Its stock had sold at $60 per share in 1964. Twenty years later, the share price had barely budged. Despite heavy expenditures, the business had struggled more or less consistently. *Wrong business*, Buffett concluded. "Buy and hold" can't work if you go into the wrong business in the first place.

A look back at all the vanished and vanquished dot-com companies proves the importance of Buffett's business analysis. During those heady days, people were buying all kinds of high-tech stocks whose prices were going up exponentially. But they were ignoring the *value* of the underlying business and its long-term prospects. Investors were buying stocks based on the *action* of the stock rather than on the *quality* of the business that the stock represented.

Companies such as Global Crossing and Etoys.com were selling for more than $80 a share. Today, they are worthless. Buffett did not buy one Internet stock because, as he saw it, these were not predictable, profitable businesses with strong balance sheets and cash flows. His business analysis told him not to go near these types of companies with a 10-foot pole.

How does Buffett determine which businesses to buy? He looks for four main things:

1. Businesses he can understand

2. Companies with favorable long-term prospects

3. Businesses operated by honest and competent people

4. Businesses priced very attractively

A conservative football coach once explained his dislike for the passing game by saying that when a football is passed, three things can happen, and two of them are bad. Buffett has the same aversion when it comes to businesses he does not understand. His business approach is safe, conservative, and unglamorous—but very effective.

Buffett likes easy-to-understand businesses because he knows that their future is more certain and their cash flows are easier to predict. Companies such as See's Candies, the Nebraska Furniture Mart, and Coca-Cola are some of his favorites because they are stable companies with predictable cash flows and earnings that likely will be doing the same thing 50 years from now.

If you can't make those kinds of predictions with confidence, says Buffett, you are *speculating* rather than investing. Sure, investing involves uncertainty. The goal is to eliminate as much uncertainty as possible in part by going into businesses that are reasonably easy to "decode." Candy and Coke lend themselves to a kind of analysis that, say, broadband capacity does not.

Buffett avoids complex companies that are subject to dramatic change because of their uncertain futures. Earnings and cash flow are two of the pillars of a successful company. An enormous capitalization—although impressive—quickly can turn into a will-o-the-wisp. Market caps matter because they are one measure of a company's clout and borrowing power. But cash in the door, quarter after quarter into the foreseeable future, matters far more.

Some might criticize Buffett for not venturing into exciting new businesses. If so, he probably would not be offended. *The bird in the hand*, he might reply, *is worth two in the bush*. Better to take the good-and-known return than the potentially-enormous-but-highly-speculative return. Better to hit singles and doubles on a regular basis than to strike out swinging for the fences.

> **Search for certainty in uncertain markets— businesses that are likely to outperform their peers over the long run.**

In many cases, says Buffett, the past is the best indicator of the future. This may sound strange to some people. Haven't we heard about the accelerating pace of change and about how the economy of the future will be enormously different from that of the past? Buffett doesn't necessarily disagree with this assessment; he just doesn't make investments based on that kind of thinking. *Look for a business that's doing the same thing today that it was doing a decade ago,* he says. Why? Well, for one thing, it's had plenty of time to figure out how to do it right. And second, that business—Buffett often points to See's Candy as an example—has found a niche within which things don't change very fast. Assuming that this stays true in the future, the company is unlikely to make any major blunders.

Is the product durable? Ask yourself the following question, even though it may sound silly at first: Which is more likely to be here in 10 years—a particular software application or a particular type of soft ice cream from Dairy Queen? The answer should be obvious: the ice cream. Software is simply moving too fast to be a good bet 10 years out.

If you don't have a good idea of what the business is going to be like in 10 years, then you do not understand the business. If you don't understand a business into which you're putting money, you are speculating rather than investing. You are hoping rather than thinking.

Here are a few things investors can do to help their long-term prospects:

Remember that a stock is a piece of a business. Don't buy a stock because of its price action; buy a stock based on analysis of the business and its future prospects.

Evaluate the fundamentals of the business before you buy any stock. Profits, earnings, cash flow, balance sheets, and income statements—these are a few of the keys that can help you to determine the long-term health of any business.

Use the Internet to do your homework. Even a few years ago, investigating a company and its prospects would have taken days or weeks—and might even have been impossible for the nonprofessional investor. Not so today; today, there are hundreds of free Web sites that reveal all types of information about a company, such as annual reports, earnings, Security and Exchange Commission (SEC) filings, cash flow, and so on.

Don't think about "stock in the short term." Think about "business in the long term."

CHAPTER 6

☑ Look for a Company That Is a Franchise

Some businesses are what Warren Buffett calls "franchises." They have high walls and deep moats around them. They are more or less unassailable. *These are the businesses you want to find.*

Warren Buffett wants to buy businesses that have enduring competitive advantages and products. He looks for companies that dominate their markets. To describe his business ideal, he employs the metaphor of a massive, impregnable castle surrounded by a deep protective moat.

Companies built like strong castles are what Buffett calls "franchises." By this he means not a franchise like a Dunkin' Donuts or a Burger King, but an entity that has a privileged position that almost guarantees its success. An "economic franchise" provides a product or service that is

1. Needed or desired

2. Not overly capital-intensive

3. Seen by its customers as having no close substitute

4. Not subject to price regulation

See's Candies, mentioned earlier, is an example of such a franchise. It's a company with a durable competitive advantage. It has been selling candy successfully for more than 70 years and most likely will be selling candy for the next 70 years.

See's products stand out from all its competitors (can you name a competitor?), and people buy See's candy because of its reputation and quality. Customers are willing to pay a premium for its products, eschewing cheaper alternatives in favor of the real thing. So your goal, as an investor, is to try to buy businesses that are franchises.

Many would-be investors begin their search by asking a question such as the following: *"How much is this company, in this industry, going to change the world?"* Buffett feels that this is missing the point in a fundamental way. Yes, a product that is "needed or desired" (criterion 1 above) is likely to have at least *some* power to change the world or part of it. But far more important, says Buffett, is figuring out whether this company has a competitive advantage that's sustainable. It is better to own See's Candies—which doesn't set out to change the world—than DeLorean Motors, which briefly tried to cross swords with Detroit. See's has a moat; DeLorean didn't—and is now long gone.

> **Search out the fortress-like firms. Find companies that stand out from their competitors.**

Buffett didn't always understand the importance of the franchise. Earlier in his career, he was far more focused on "great buys"—which turned out to be bad buys in the long run. Buffett bought himself an expensive education in the unappealing economics of farm equipment manufacturers, second-tier department stores, and New England textile mills. Not a strong wall or a deep moat among them!

In 1965, Buffett bought the New England textile company Berkshire Hathaway. Twenty years later, he closed down the textile operation of Berkshire Hathaway because it had no future and was losing money. Global competitors were killing this piece of the company, and—with no long-lasting competitive advantage and no moat to safeguard its prospects—the textile business eventually crumbled.

Compare those early mistakes with what Buffett did in 2003, when he shocked many observers by buying about 2 billion shares of Chinese oil company PetroChina. This huge company, which many people had never heard of, dominates the oil business in China, is the fourth most profitable oil company in the world, and produces as much crude oil as Exxon. This is the type of business stronghold to add to your portfolio when you are fortunate enough to find it.

One other key to buying franchises—or any business—is to wait until the company is reasonably priced. This has been a hallmark of Buffett's methodology.

> **Do not dart in and out of the market. Research shows that frequent trading leads to mounting losses.**

One Buffett expert and author, Timothy Vick, suggests that you make a list of your favorite companies and also the top prices that you would be willing to pay for them. Keep the list close by and monitor it every so often. This will help you to maintain discipline while allowing you to avoid moves that will hurt your portfolio.

In Vick's best-selling book, *How to Pick Stocks Like Warren Buffett* (for the sake of full disclosure, this book also is published by McGraw-Hill), he makes a very compelling argument for "warehousing stocks" as Buffett does: ". . . it forces you to be vigilant. Before buying, you must determine a reasonable value of the company, which means studying the enterprise. Putting some time into the valuation process will greatly decrease your chances of buying prematurely" (p. 98).

Here are some suggestions for helping you to pick and hold the right companies:

Search out the franchises that will stand the test of time. Always be on the lookout for companies that meet Buffett's criteria: a company that produces products that are needed or desired, that has no close substitutes, that does not eat up capital, and that is not subject to price regulation.

Study companies' underlying fundamentals before you buy them. Make sure that you are doing the right due diligence before making stock purchases. This will help you to make better investment decisions and increase your prospects of success over the long haul.

Don't hesitate to "take strikes" before you swing. Buffett advocates taking strikes. That's baseball parlance for a batter who lets some balls get by before swinging at them. Over time, the best investors make fewer and fewer buy and sell decisions.

If you see piranhas and crocodiles in a big moat surrounding a big castle, says Buffett, you have the type of long-lasting business that can reward investors.

CHAPTER 7

✓ Buy Low-Tech, Not High-Tech

In Buffett's world, successful investing is rarely a gee-whiz activity. It's less often about rockets and lasers and more often about things such as brick, carpets, paint, and insulation.

Warren Buffett has bought a brick company, a paint company, a carpet company, several furniture companies, and an underwear company. These are the kinds of businesses Buffett loves to own because they are all easy-to-understand, stable businesses with predictable cash flows. They are nothing fancy or glamorous—just good, solid companies that don't change much over the years. They deliver consistent earnings and revenue growth year after year.

Buffett does not own any exotic or "new economy" companies on the cutting edge of technology, such as fiberoptics, computer software, or biotech. All too often, he says, the returns on these exotic technologies don't go to the investors who first made them possible. He cites industries like radio and television, which certainly changed our lives—but didn't reward their investors.

What kind of girl will you invite to the prom? Will you invite the exotic newcomer to town, whom everybody thinks is dazzling, but no one really knows very much about? Or will you invite the girl next door? *Go with the girl next door,* says Buffett. Don't fall under the spell of a "sexy" new business with alluring growth prospects. The very same factors that make it sexy also make reliable evaluations of its long-term economics very difficult. Yes, a glamorous business may have spectacular short-term success, but, ultimately, it is likely to flop.

What about those brick, paint, carpet, and furniture companies—those "girl next door" companies? Most likely they'll be around for the next 100 years because they are businesses whose products are highly unlikely to become obsolete. They are all companies that have a long-term competitive advantage and consistent earnings power. *Think 30 years,* advises Buffett. *Thirty years of performance makes for a great company. Three years does not.*

Etoys.com, Cyberrebate.com, Webvan.com, Kozmo .com, Pets.com, Planetrx.com, Rx.com, and Pandesic .com—what do all these companies have in common?

They all were amazing high-tech successes for about a year or two. They all enjoyed brief success, and then they all failed. Webvan.com, an online grocery delivery company, had a market capitalization of $7.5 *billion* before it went bankrupt. Breathtaking? Absolutely. Great investments? Not unless you flipped them almost immediately. Hundreds of billions of dollars of shareholder wealth went up in smoke virtually overnight.

High tech may well be fine, says Buffett—for other people. But when Buffett can't figure out who in an industry is going to make money or how, he stays away. Conversely, when he understands the revenue stream, he's far more likely to buy in. He is *disciplined*. If he does not understand the business, or if it is too complex or hard to predict, he will keep his money in his pocket. This discipline is very important in trying to implement Buffett's value investment philosophy. Be wary of exotic businesses that have an air of quick and easy riches to them. And if big changes appear to be on a company's horizon, stay away. If you can't tell *exactly how and when* this company is going to make money—at least to your satisfaction—stay away.

Buffett once analyzed a 1988 *Fortune* magazine investor's guide that assessed the performance of 1,000 big companies. He noted that the best performers were mostly mundane businesses. It was a clear case of the tortoise and the hare. And just as in the fable, *the tortoise won*. The boring companies beat the sexy, glamorous ones.

> **Do not be tempted by get-rich-quick deals involving relatively complex companies (e.g., high-tech companies). They are the most unpredictable in the long run.**

Investing in a high-tech company is like a quarterback throwing the ball 60 yards downfield. Every now and then there will be spectacular results and great gains, but most of the time the pass will go uncompleted. Buffett prefers to run the ball up the middle for a guaranteed three yards and a cloud full of profits. It's a lot like the Vince Lombardi approach to coaching the Green Bay Packers: *Better to be certain of a good result than hopeful of a great one.*

Here are three ways to refine your investing strategy:

Avoid businesses in changing industries. One of Buffett's keys is buying companies that he understands with predictable business models and earnings growth. Do not give in to the "siren's song" of hip Silicon Valley companies. Those businesses are simply too hard to predict over the long haul. If you're in doubt, visit the cemetery of dot-com businesses; this will underscore the dangers of investing in exciting companies that promise off-the-charts growth.

Invest in "old economy" businesses. Buffett loves the boring and mundane. This is so because these businesses likely will be in the same business decades hence.

Look at businesses that have been around the last 50 years to help you to figure out which will survive the next 50 years.

Remember that it takes decades for companies to become great. The last lesson of this Buffett strategy is to think long term. There are simply too many companies that go up like a rocket in their first years only to fall like a stone a few years down the road. Try to winnow out the businesses that might be "disrupted" by a new technology or competitor.

Look for the absence of change. Look for the business whose only change in the future will be doing more business.

CHAPTER 8

☑ Concentrate Your Stock Investments

Avoid what Buffett calls the "Noah's Ark" style of investing—that is, a little of this, a little of that. Better to have a smaller number of investments with more of your money in each.

Most "experts" tell investors to diversify—that is, to own many equities at one time—so that if one particular stock plummets, it won't drag down your whole portfolio. Warren Buffett goes more or less in the opposite direction.

Diversification, the practice of owning shares in many different companies, according to Buffett, is not necessarily the right way to invest. Buffett's policy is to concentrate his holdings. He likes to have only a few holdings and to invest a lot of money into them. If you've found the right stock, why buy only a little? He subscribes to Mae West's philosophy that "too much of a good thing is wonderful."

Buffett's endorsement of concentration—and conversely, his rejection of diversification—is another key clue to his investment philosophy. It should come as no surprise by now that it goes against the prevailing wisdom of Wall Street.

Most brokers recommend that you diversify your investment portfolio. "Don't put all your eggs in one basket," they advise. "Hedge your bets." They would rather have you be like Noah and hold two shares of every conceivable company. Buffett disagrees. Buy 5 to 10 good companies at a bargain price and buy as large a position in each as you can. Why put money into your twentieth-best choice, asks Buffett, rather than your top five or ten?

When Buffett feels strongly about an investment, he does not hold back. In fact, he tends to invest huge sums in it. For example, he invested $1 billion in Coca-Cola stock, ultimately purchasing 200 million shares. He purchased 151 million American Express shares. He purchased more than 2 billion shares of PetroChina—the Chinese oil company—at a cost of $488 million. That holding, incidentally, is now worth more than $1.2 billion.

In 2004, Berkshire Hathaway had significant investments in only 10 publicly traded companies. At other

> **When you are convinced of a strong business's prospects, be aggressive and add to your position rather than buying the fifteenth or twentieth stock on your list of possible investments.**

times, it has had major holdings in as few as 5. Buffett has demonstrated repeatedly that when you buy a lot of shares in the right business at the right price, this strategy—a strategy of concentration—can work wonders over time.

Charlie Munger, Berkshire Hathaway's vice chairman, also strongly believes in nondiversification. In fact, he goes a step farther, arguing that "in the United States, a person or institution with almost all wealth invested, long-term, in just three fine domestic corporations is securely rich." It's patience and nondiversification, says Munger, that explain the astounding success of Buffett and Berkshire Hathaway.

So when brokers urge you to diversify your holdings and warn you that too much wealth in a few stocks puts you at significant risk and with a very unbalanced portfolio, keep in mind that Warren Buffett is presently worth over $44 billion because he directly owns 474,998 shares in one single company, Berkshire Hathaway. Benjamin Graham's GEICO Insurance holding was similarly responsible for most of his wealth. Munger believes that when the opportunity to get into a "wonderful business run by a wonderful manager" arises, it's a big mistake not to load up.

Why not wait to find a great company at a great price and make a substantial investment in it instead of investing diluted amounts in 27 mutual funds or 27 different stocks?

How can you take advantage of this Buffett strategy? Try these three to-do items:

When putting together your stock portfolio, aim to own no more than 10 stocks. Buffett believes that despite what the experts say, diversification can increase your chances of subpar returns. Do your homework and find 5 to 10 stocks that you would want to own for the next 5 to 10 years. Then wait until they hit your price point. When they do, buy them with confidence and—perhaps most important—have patience.

Make sure that the stocks you buy fit Buffett's criteria. They need to be in good, solid (even "boring") businesses that have strong management teams. Study the performance of the firm under present management. And don't get an itchy trigger finger. Wait for these companies to be priced attractively.

Be courageous. Many of Buffett's biggest investments were bravely done during economic and business downturns when almost everyone else was too scared to act.

Portfolio concentration—the opposite strategy of diversification—also has the power to focus the mind wonderfully. How? If you're putting your eggs in only a few baskets, you're far less likely to make investments on impulse or emotion.

CHAPTER 9

☑ Practice Inactivity, Not Hyperactivity

There are times when doing nothing is a sign of investing brilliance.

The energy that is expended each day on the floor of the New York Stock Exchange is truly stunning. More than a *billion shares* change hands—and that's on an average day.

This frenetic pace often gets downloaded to the other players in the investment game. There are day and swing traders buying shares today and intending to sell them a few days later; there are literally thousands of mutual funds and other financial institutions behaving like whirling dervishes, feverishly tweaking their portfolios daily, weekly, and monthly.

Even the individual investor is affected. One of the common myths about investing that has arisen over time is that you must trade frequently to be successful. But there is at least one legendary investor who is a notable exception to all this hyperactivity. Warren Buffett, arguably the greatest investor of all time, looks more like Rip Van Winkle than a whirling dervish. He refers to inactivity as "intelligent behavior." He says, accurately, that the wise investor can make money while snoring. He applauds lethargy and refers to it as a cornerstone of his investment philosophy.

Lethargy? Inactivity? Snoring your way to riches? What's going on here? Isn't investing all about life in the fast lane?

In a word, "No." Buffett shuns what he calls "hyperactivity." No move is a good move if you already own the right stocks. A review in 2004 of Buffett's six largest holdings revealed that he had last changed his position in Moody's in 2000, in American Express in 1998, in Coca-Cola in 1994, in Gillette in 1989, and in the Washington Post Company way back in 1973. Not exactly a pattern to endear Buffett to brokers!

Buffett likes to buy stocks, but selling is a different story. He likens the sales-prone investor to a bee flitting from flower to flower. If you're already on the right flower, he advises, *stay there*. Resist the temptations of hyperactivity.

Buffett has achieved success by being patient and *in*active. Most investors are highly impatient and hyperactive. Buffett believes such frequent trading to be hazardous to your wealth. Frequent trading results in

+ mistakes

frictional costs, such as commissions and capital gains taxes, whereas inactive long-term ownership of a stock avoids these costs.

> **Do not trade for trading's sake. Frequent trading is the hallmark of overactive investors, who tend to wind up with more losses than gains.**

The tax implications of frequent trading are over-looked by many investors. Buffett hammers away on this theme, pointing out that given the same compounded rate of return, the tax-paying individual (as most of us are!) is *far better off* sticking with one stock than going in and out of many. Taxable events kill net returns to investors.

John C. Bogle—the legendary founder of the Vanguard family of mutual funds and a great Buffett fan—is in the same camp. He has spent more than half a century warning everyone who would listen about the hidden costs of investing. In addition to commissions and taxes, Bogle says, there are other costs associated with investing that most individual investors are not aware of.

For example, any "load" (commission-based) mutual fund not only charges several percentage points of commission but also inherent in the price of those shares are trading costs, activity costs, and so on. Like taxes, these hidden costs eat away at net returns to the investor in the long run—but most investors don't even know that they are being charged these fees. The more trading, says Bogle, the more losses. He likens frequent trading to gambling in Las Vegas: The house always wins in the end.

For great investors like Bogle and Buffett, inactivity means infrequent buying and selling, but it also means something else: waiting as long as necessary for a buying opportunity to appear. If there is a year that does not present an opportunity, Buffett just hunkers down and waits patiently for the next opportunity to arrive, however long it takes. In 2004, Buffett did not make any major investments. Several years ago Buffett estimated that in something like 50 of the 61 years that he had been investing, there were good opportunities to be found. Looked at from the other perspective, this means that in almost one year out of five—20 percent of the time—there was *nothing worth buying*. If you can't remember the last time you let a whole year go by without buying something, you may be doing something wrong.

How can you be sure that you are not getting caught up in market fever and trading too frequently? Try these Buffett tenets:

Be a decades trader, not a day or swing trader. Remember the style of Buffett Van Winkle! The key to investing is coming out a winner in the long run. Own great companies for a long time and you will outperform the vast majority of more active investors.

Don't mistake activity for achievement. Buffett is committed to living this tenet, popularized by the great

UCLA coach John Wooden. Don't get stampeded. Don't join the anxious multitudes who trade for the sake of trading. If you find yourself doing that, find yourself another hobby!

Beware of hidden costs. When it comes to investing, few things are free. You can help yourself in the long run, however, by sidestepping costs and minimizing taxes. This means not paying hefty commissions on stock or mutual fund transactions. It means avoiding frequent trades. It means being patient and allowing money to compound. It means asking lots of questions, reading prospectuses of stocks and funds, and not acting on that hot tip you picked up on the talk-radio show or over the back-yard fence. Stick with your plan.

When in doubt, be lethargic. Better to practice your snoring than to spin your wheels and incur costs.

CHAPTER 10

☑ Don't Look at the Ticker

Tickers are all about prices. Investing is about a lot more than prices.

Does the world's greatest investor own a modern stock ticker? *No.* So how does Warren Buffett track hourly or daily stock-price movements? *He doesn't.* How about monthly or yearly movements? *Not particularly interested.*

Contrast this to any brokerage office or financial news TV program, where stock quotes run across the screen in an endless streaming barrage of prices, numbers, and decimals. Many "active investors" (those who trade stocks often) watch these moment-by-moment price movements as if their lives depended on them and attach great importance to the slightest price deviation.

Question: What would a day trader be without a ticker?
Answer: Not a day trader.

Warren Buffett, the classic value investor, simply does not care what happens to price deviations in the short run. If one owns shares in great businesses, then the short term doesn't matter, and the long term will take care of itself. The only exception to this rule is if prices drop significantly, offering Buffett a chance to buy *more shares* at the depressed levels. When stocks go on sale, Buffett is interested.

Again, Buffett keeps his eye trained on how well the underlying business is doing. His focus is on the value of the business and its future prospects, not on the stock price. For most people, the focus is the other way around, manifested by an obsession to constantly check prices and day-to-day trading volume.

But this is a formula for driving you crazy rather than a recipe for investment success. Checking the price every day can lead to exaggerated mood swings: An increase in the share price elicits elation, whereas a fall in the price causes a sense of gloom and doom. And when these mood swings start affecting your buying and selling decisions, all sorts of bad things can start to happen.

> **Wean yourself. Shun the ticker. Abstain from looking at share prices every day.**

Buffett claims that he hasn't had a quote on See's Candies since he first bought it in 1972—more than three decades ago—and he doesn't need one. He points out that people somehow make it through the weekend without their stock-price "fixes." The sophisticated investor, he says, wouldn't even miss the stock market if it closed down for a year or two. If you have your portfolio solidly in place, why fret over price fluctuations?

Instead of focusing on the price movements of his stock, an investor's time would be better served by monitoring the *performance of the business*: its management, earnings, cash flow, future prospects, and so on. Did you know that in 1960, Wal-Mart had sales of $1.4 million and profits of $112,000? In 1980, sales were $1.2 billion, and profits were $41 million. In 1990, sales rose to $26 billion with profits of $1 billion. This is what Buffett finds important. The stock price will *eventually* reflect the value of the business. But that future price will be driven not by today's hysteria but by tomorrow's earnings. He makes an analogy to being a spectator at a ball game. The point is to *watch the field of play* rather than the scoreboard. What does the quality of your team's play say about its prospects in the latter innings? And where's the best place to look for those prospects? *On the field itself.*

It's *performance* that counts. Consider the following: If you had bought 100 Wal-Mart shares in 1970 for $16.50 a share, 20 years later this investment would have been worth an unbelievable total of 51,200 shares (the result of nine two-for-one stock splits) at a price of $62 a share—in other words, $1,650 turned into more than

$3.1 million (from Sam Walton's book, *Made in America,* Bantam Books, New York, 1993). Intoxicating, right? But *it didn't happen because people were watching stock tickers; it happened because a business turned in a spectacular performance.*

If you buy shares in a great business, in other words, the stock market ticker ultimately will validate your choice. As Ben Graham said, "In the short run, the market is a voting machine, but in the long run, it is a weighing machine."

To invest like Buffett, *change your habits.* Get in the habit of judging the success of your investment on the performance of the business—and not on the performance of the stock.

Berkshire Hathaway generates $100 million a week in cash through its business operations. The business continues to perform well, management is strong, and its future prospects look bright. So who really cares what the ticker is saying about the price of Berkshire Hathaway today? If the business is strong, the ticker will reflect that strength over the long term. So look at the *operating results* of your companies. Eventually, the markets will assess your investments in exactly the same terms. The hysterias of the moment will subside, the strong companies will emerge, and their prices will be high.

What can you do to develop Buffett-like investing habits. Consider doing the following:

Turn off the noise. If you are a daily watcher of investment shows—those shows practically overflowing with hot tips delivered by supposedly expert "talking heads"—*turn them off.* Again, wean yourself. This is background noise. The key is not daily price movements but the health of the businesses you are considering owning.

Study the playing field and not the scoreboard. Shift your focus from prices to fundamentals—things such as cash flow, balance sheets, and future earnings. This is what will determine stock prices in the long run. And if you're an investor—rather than a trader—only the long term matters.

Know the value of something rather than the price of everything. The legendary Phillip Fisher once said that the stock market was "filled with individuals who know the price of everything but the value of nothing." Do not fall into this trap; focus on value, *not* price.

Warren Buffett doesn't know what his own company—Berkshire Hathaway—is selling for today. He doesn't know and doesn't much care what it was selling for yesterday or will sell for tomorrow. He *does* care what it will be selling for a decade from now—because that will be a measure of the company's performance and therefore its true value.

CHAPTER 11

☑ View Market Downturns as Buying Opportunities

Market downturns aren't body blows; they are buying opportunities. If the herd starts running away from a good stock, get ready to run toward it.

A typical newspaper article in the summer of 2004 reported that the Dow Jones Industrial Average had "plunged nearly 150 points" to a new 2004 low as investors "bailed out of stocks in the wake of a disappointing jobs report and continuing high oil prices" and "sold off heavily for a second straight day" because of worries about inflation and slow job growth, which threatened to "interrupt the economic recovery for a sustained length of time."

And so on and so on. Take the numbers out of the preceding paragraph, and it could serve as a template for any number of articles over the past several decades. Bad things happen out there in the world, and markets fall. Then good things happen, and markets rise.

Then they fall again, and Wall Street—and the industry around Wall Street—panics. "Panic" is a word that has been banished from Wall Street's vocabulary, but the reality of the panic mentality is still there. Most people with money in the stock market hate it when stock prices fall. They view market corrections as setbacks at best and as disasters at worst. When they lose their nerve, they "cut their losses" and bail out of the market.

When markets plunge, however, there is *at least* one investor who is not selling his shares and running for the exits. Warren Buffett, once again, presents a stark contrast to the prevailing wisdom of Wall Street. Most people sell at exactly the wrong time—when prices are falling. Buffett *loves* it when stock prices plunge because it presents buying opportunities. By extension, he says, savvy investors should learn to get comfortable with market volatility. If we never experienced wild swings—if we *didn't* have those plunges that give Wall Street fits—we would never get large opportunities opening up.

Most of Buffett's greatest investments were made either during bear markets when share prices of great businesses had plummeted (along with everything else) or when great companies were experiencing temporary but surmountable difficulties and their share prices became depressed.

Washington Post, GEICO, and Wells Fargo are examples of how Buffett pounces on market downturns to invest for the future. In 1973, the stock market was way down, lowering the price of shares in the *Washington Post* to about $6 each, adjusted for later stock splits. Buffett pounced, pouring $10.6 million into the company.

More than 30 years later, the price of that $6 share is now more than $900, the second most expensive share on the New York Stock Exchange after Berkshire Hathaway itself. Again, Buffett bought into a solid business when its shares were selling at a tremendous discount. This is what Buffett does so well. He constantly searches for underpriced shares whose values are higher than their prices, akin to buying dollar bills for 40 cents.

> **Search for quality businesses that go "on sale" for reasons other than the underlying fundamentals of the business or the quality of its management.**

Owing to the whims of the financial markets, so often controlled by greed or fear, shares of excellent businesses sometimes will sink in price, presenting a great opportunity to buy bargain-priced shares. In other words, the irrationality of the market gets attached to businesses that shouldn't be tarred by the same brush—but are. This is a pouncing opportunity.

In 1976, GEICO shares had plummeted from $61 to $2. The company was on very shaky financial ground, to say the least. Buffett was convinced that GEICO would recover because it had a great business franchise, a defensible competitive advantage in the insurance business, and strong management.

Consequently, Buffett started to accumulate GEICO shares, ultimately investing $46 million in the company. GEICO had been "misappraised" in Buffett's eyes; all he had to do was make his investment and wait for a more accurate appraisal to be made. As noted earlier, that reappraisal ultimately came. His $46 million stake turned into a *billion-dollar* stake.

In 1990, Buffett bought 5 million shares of Wells Fargo Bank at a time when banks were getting hammered, thanks to a recent history of shaky loan-making and a poor business climate. Wells Fargo in particular was having problems because of the depressed California real estate market. But Buffett liked Wells Fargo. He liked its management team, he liked the business, and he particularly liked the depressed stock price.

The moral of these stories—and many more like them—is that Buffett bought many shares when great businesses were selling at a discount owing to market and business conditions. Almost every strong business is going to encounter difficulty at some point, and its share price is going to drop. This is often the best time to buy, because eventually the stock market will recognize the value of the company, and the stock price will catch up.

As Buffett's mentor Ben Graham wrote: "The investor who permits himself to be stampeded or unduly worried by the unjustified market declines in his holdings is perversely transforming his basic advantage into a basic disadvantage. Price fluctuations have only one significant meaning for the true investor. They provide him with an opportunity to buy wisely when prices fall sharply and to sell wisely when they advance a great deal."

How do you inject some of the Buffett magic into your own investing techniques? Consider the following:

Change your investing mind-set. Reprogram your thinking. Learn to *like* a sinking market because it presents opportunity. Do not get caught up with the masses and hit the panic button when markets fall.

Always search for value. Buffett's greatest investments were made when share prices were depressed owing to market conditions or to a company experiencing temporary difficulty. The key is to recognize the difference between a temporary setback and a real fatal flaw in a company.

Pounce when the three Buffett variables come together. When a strong business with an enduring competitive advantage, strong management, and a low stock price comes onto your investment screen, *pounce*—even if you start with only a limited number of shares.

Buffett says that investors don't lose when markets fall—only "disinvestors." So be like Buffett: Be an investor.

CHAPTER 12

☑ Don't Swing at Every Pitch

What if you had to predict how every stock in the Standard & Poor's (S&P) 500 would do over the next few years? In this scenario, Warren Buffett—one of the greatest investors of all time—doesn't like his chances. But what if your job was to find only *one stock* among those 500 that would do well? In this revised scenario, Buffett now likes his odds, which he figures at something like 9 in 10.

According to many self-professed stock market experts, to be a successful investor means making a large number of investment decisions in one's lifetime. Warren Buffett does not agree. In fact, he says, one good decision a year is a very high standard—hard to clear but high enough to guarantee success.

Buffett likes to use a baseball analogy to describe his way of investing. An investor is standing at the plate, and potential stock market investments are pitched continuously across the plate. *Don't swing at every pitch,* says Buffett.

Instead, be patient, let pitches go by, and wait for the *right* pitch. Buffett read *The Science of Hitting*, by legendary Red Sox batsman Ted Williams, with great interest. To the nonexpert, the strike zone is a strike zone, and you swing at whatever looks hittable. But Williams saw the strike zone as a large landscape that had to be carved up into many smaller zones. Only when the pitch came into a very small subzone—a "sweet spot"—would Williams swing at it.

Buffett is always at the plate watching pitches go by. But he only swings at pitches—at stocks—that cross the plate in the sweet spot. His sweet spot, as noted earlier, is the great business with a strong earnings future, led by capable and ethical management, and available at a good stock price. If the pitches are not in the sweet spot and do not meet these criteria, he does not swing.

And, as noted, he might wait for a couple of years before making an investment because he does not like any of the businesses coming across the plate. He has let years go buy without swinging. Only when all these ingredients are present will Buffett swing—and then he swings mightily, investing a lot of money. Buffett's result? For him, it is usually a grand slam.

> **There's the investing equivalent of the strike zone—and also the investing equivalent of the "sweet spot."**

Buffett feels that one of his biggest mistakes was not investing heavily in Wal-Mart stock. He believes that he could have made at least $10 billion if he had swung at Wal-Mart, but he did not like the share price at the time. Buffett call this and similar misjudgments "mistakes of omission"—a mistake that resulted from a failure to swing at a particular pitch. But Buffett easily forgives himself for these kinds of mistakes. He's harder on himself for mistakes of commission, that is, investing heavily in a stock that turns out poorly.

One of Buffett's rare mistakes of commission was investing in US Air, where he learned the hard way about the airline business. From Buffett's perspective, forgoing a $10 billion win with Wal-Mart probably hurts less than losing a smaller amount on US Air. A mistake of omission reflects discipline in action; a mistake of commission reflects a breakdown of that discipline. And, overall, it must be noted, Buffett's batting average is more than respectable. In the four decades that Buffett has run Berkshire Hathaway, its gains have exceeded its losses by a ratio of *100 to 1*.

In fact, Buffett is the Ted Williams of Wall Street. A year-by-year examination of Buffett's stock market investments from 1987 to 2004 reveals that almost every one of his investments—almost every pitch he has swung at—has increased tremendously in value. For example, his $463 million Wells Fargo investment is now worth $3.5 billion. His $1.4 billion investment in American Express is now worth $8.5 billion.

As an investor, if you are disciplined, if you wait for a company with a great business and great management and it is selling at a discounted price, swing for the fences if you have the means to do so and can tolerate the risk.

You only have to swing a couple of times in your investing lifetime to be successful. Charlie Munger says that if you took the top 15 investments out of Berkshire Hathaway's portfolio, you'd be left with a pretty average performance. The lesson? You can't usually hit a bad pitch out of the park—and you can hit a good pitch a long way.

Warren Buffett recommends that people keep a mental punch card on which they are allowed only 20 investment decisions in a lifetime. Every time they make an investment decision, that counts as one punch. Buffett believes that this punch-card idea will force people to think carefully and for a long time before making an investment. This will improve the chances of a successful outcome while eliminating hasty and impulsive decisions. It's quality—not quantity—that should govern your investment strategy.

How can you increase your odds of investment success? Try these on for size:

Adapt Buffett's punch-card idea to your own portfolio. Impose discipline in your every move by allowing only a certain number of investments. Make every one count by doing your homework, watching the fundamentals, and being patient.

Make sure that the pitch is in the sweet spot. Remember that Buffett's sweet spot has three parts: great businesses with a strong earnings future, led by capable and ethical management, and available at a good stock price.

Don't swing too soon. In addition to limiting the number of trades you make, make sure that you "enter a position" (buy a stock) when the time is right. Remember, Buffett sometimes has waited years before pulling the trigger on a particular business.

A few good investments are all that is needed.

CHAPTER 13

✓ **Ignore the Macro; Focus on the Micro**

According to Warren Buffett, the big things—the large trends that are external to the business—don't matter. It's the *little* things, the things that are *business-specific*, that count.

Do you know that Warren Buffett, arguably the world's greatest investor, doesn't let macroeconomic factors affect his decisions? He's not a "macro guy," as he puts it. If the Fed chairman were whispering in his left ear and the Secretary of the Treasury were whispering in his right, revealing their vision of the future, he wouldn't be listening. He'd be *watching his businesses*.

Think about it: The conventional approach is to rely a great deal on macro events when making investment decisions. Things like economic indicators, growth of the economy, housing starts, and political events loom large in most investors' minds. The cable news programs are full of financial analysis and advice based on macro events.

For example, a typical business news report from the spring of 2004 included the following: "Watch for the market to move within a range, especially in light of the Democratic and Republican National Conventions, the Summer Olympics, and the ongoing tension in Iraq. These rallies will likely lack momentum, so take your profits where you can or have your stop losses in place."

In that same time period, another television pundit observed, "Apprehension regarding Senator John Kerry's tax policy, the risk of terrorism, high oil prices, and the outcome of the presidential election are creating uncertainty and skittishness in the market."

All in all, this is quite a laundry list of factors to have to weigh, right? Buffett's advice: *Don't bother*. Focus on the tree rather than on the forest. Don't concern yourself with the short-term fate of the stock market; concern yourself with the long-term prospects of the businesses in which you're invested (or in which you propose to invest). If you spend time worrying about where the market is going to be a month or a year from now, says Buffett, that's simply time wasted.

Ask yourself what, exactly, are you analyzing. Are you an analyst of the national economy? An analyst of the market? A "securities analyst"? If you answered "yes" to any of these questions, says Buffett, you got it wrong. You are, or should be, a *business analyst*.

To invest like Buffett, you need to ignore macro factors and events and really concentrate on the companies in which you are considering investing. Analyze the business prospects, the management team, and so on. "Putting the blinders on" usually has bad connotations— in other words, that you're not thinking broadly enough. But when it comes to analyzing things, Buffett advises, *put those blinders on*. Don't get distracted by macro issues.

Think back to the lessons of earlier chapters. As a Buffett-style investor, you spend a great deal of time arriving at an informed opinion about a company. It makes no sense to substitute an uninformed opinion (a "guess") about the economy for your hard-earned wisdom about a particular company. Trust that wisdom!

Buffett likes to catalog all the externalities that have taken place since he started his investment career—such things as the deep involvement of the United States in the Vietnam war, the imposition of wage and price controls by a conservative Republican president, the resignation of that president, multiple oil shocks, the collapse of the Soviet Union, a 508-point drop in the Dow in one day, a prime rate approaching 20 percent, and Treasury bill yields fluctuating between 2.8 and 17.4 percent. No one, says Buffett, had a good enough crystal ball to predict these events. And none of these dramatic events had *any impact* on Buffett's approach to investing.

In fact, says Buffett, some of his best purchases came in the wake of events that scared other investors away from the market. Even after the horrible events of September 11, 2001, Buffett did not sell any shares; rather, he indicated that he might *buy* shares if market prices dropped significantly. His was a lonely position in those tragic days—but a wise one. Buffett predicts that the next several decades will hold their share of disasters—natural and otherwise—but he sees absolutely no reason to stop buying "first-class businesses" when the opportunity arises.

To put on your own set of "Buffett blinders," consider the following:

Don't pretend to be an economist if you're not one. Your job as an investor is not to analyze all the numbers being reported by the government. As a rule, you shouldn't let your investment decisions be influenced by macroeconomic factors and political events.

Don't panic. Buffett is not naive. He understands that we live in a different age after the events of September 11, 2001 (and March 11, 2004, in Spain). He understands that some events, such as terrorism and war, can affect stock prices in the near term. But he *does not panic*. In the weeks and months following September 11, 2001, the financial markets took a beating. But three years later, the Standard & Poor's (S&P) 500 was recording new multiyear highs. Had you panicked at that time—and plenty of investors did—you would have bailed out of the market at *exactly the wrong point* in the cycle. Don't panic!

Macro events can create opportunities. While your primary focus should not be on the macro, keep an eye out for the opportunities that some events might bring. Every so often something on the outside, the macro, will have a direct effect on the micro, the price of a stock. To that extent, you should keep an eye on things so that you recognize when a stock price plummets because of an external event.

It's possible, admits Buffett, to imagine a cataclysm so terrible that the markets would collapse and not bounce back. (He points to the use of weapons of mass destruction by terrorists as one such scenario.) But other than that, Buffett says, the externalities don't matter—and you can't predict them, anyway. Focus on what you *can* know: the workings of a good business.

CHAPTER 14

☑ Take a Close Look at Management

The analysis begins—and sometimes ends— with one key question: *Who's in charge here?*

Warren Buffett looks for great businesses that also have great management—and, as summed up earlier, he won't invest until both factors (great competitive position and great management) are in place. Therefore, as an investor, it is very important for you to closely evaluate the management team of any prospective business in which you are thinking of investing.

There are several key factors to scrutinize as you begin your assessment:

1. Is the management team working for share-holders, or is it working to enrich itself at share-

holders' expense (e.g., through excessive salaries, bonuses, options, and expensive perks)?

2. Is management frugal, or is it overweighted with spendthrifts?

3. Is management dedicated to improving shareholder value and the rational allocation of capital?

4. Does management repurchase shares for the benefit of shareholders and avoid issuing new shares that dilute shareholder ownership?

5. Are shareholders treated as partners or patsies?

6. Is the company's annual report candid and straightforward or fluff?

7. Does management appear to engage in honest accounting, or does it appear to be hiding information and concealing the true numbers?

At the end of the day, what were the Enron, WorldCom, and HealthSouth stories all about? They were all about the chaos and value destruction that can result when managers put their own interests above those of the business and of the shareholders. They were all about the perils to shareholders of incompetent executives. Or, to put it more positively, they were all about the importance of *ethical* and *competent* leadership. When Buffett makes an investment, he is "going into business with" that company's leaders. When you phrase it in this way, you have very little choice but to partner with individuals whom you trust and admire.

You can make a bad deal with a good person, but—says Buffett—you can't make a good deal with a bad person. Why would you even try? Your own reputation may well suffer, and your investment will be put at unnecessary risk. Entrust your money to people you trust.

In 2003, Buffett took home a salary of $100,000 from Berkshire Hathaway. In that same year, the average chief executive officer's compensation (base salary and bonuses) totaled more than $2 million. And that doesn't speak to options or other kinds of special executive perks. Most CEOs enjoyed lots of these perks; Buffett has no options, bonuses, or lavish executive perks. In fact, 99.9 percent of his wealth is in the shares of his company.

The result? Buffett makes money only when his shareholders make money. He treats shareholders as partners, and every decision he makes is made with the aim of improving shareholder value. For example, because issuing new shares dilutes the holdings of existing investors, Buffett goes that route only grudgingly and only rarely. When Buffett took control of Berkshire Hathaway in 1965, there were 1,137,778 outstanding shares. Forty years later, amazingly, the number of outstanding Berkshire Hathaway A shares is *less than 1.4 million*. At Berkshire Hathaway, frugality and cost consciousness are ingrained parts of the corporate culture.

Charlie Munger says, "The opulence at the head office is often inversely related to the financial substance of the firm." Berkshire Hathaway's corporate headquarters in Omaha are unimpressive and unglamorous (to put it kindly). If you're looking for multimillion-dollar office rehabs, don't bother looking in Buffett's corner of Omaha. On the other hand, if you're looking for *financial* substance—glamorous numbers—you've come to the right place.

Sam Walton, the founder of Wal-Mart, was famous for his frugality and lack of corporate ostentation. This is the kind of manager that Buffett loves and seeks to associate himself with. Look for managers who are more interested in cutting costs than in installing gold-plated faucets in the executive bathroom (or $6,000 shower curtains, as one infamous CEO is reported to have purchased).

So the quality of management is very important to Buffett. But good management must be married to a good business. You can be the best jockey in the world, Buffett warns, but you can't win the race riding a broken-down nag. That's the stuff of fairy tales, and fairy tales aren't the basis of good investments.

Avoid investing in poor businesses, even if they have great management. Ultimately, the quality of the business will win out—will *lose* out—and sink the investment.

Buffett has a number of warnings for investors to look out for when assessing companies and their management, especially in their annual reports. First of all, analyze their accounting. If it looks weak, stay away. If the company doesn't expense options; presents fanciful pension assumptions; trumpets its earnings *before* interest, taxes, depreciation, and amortization (EBITDA); and relies on a blizzard of unintelligible footnotes, these are all bad signs. Let's assume that you have at least a modest ability to read financial statements. If you can't understand something in a company's financial statement, says Buffett, it's because management doesn't *want* you to understand it. Do you want a business partner who hides things from you? Certainly not!

In addition, Buffett warns investors to be suspicious about companies that look exclusively to the future for their "good news." Is the good news all about earnings projections and growth expectations? *Bad sign*, says Buffett. He does so based partly on his own experience as a CEO. The senior managers at Berkshire Hathaway have no clear idea what one of their businesses is likely to earn in the coming year—or even the next quarter. When an executive claims to know the future, Buffett warns, that's a bad sign. And when an executive actually *hits* those numbers, quarter after quarter, that's a *really* bad sign. It strongly suggests that something is being manipulated somewhere. If you make ironclad commitments to "make your numbers," you may put yourself in a position where you have to make *up* the numbers— eventually leading to all kinds of mischief and unhappiness. HealthSouth did this exact thing as its CEO boasted of 46 consecutive quarters of exceeding analyst's earnings expectations before the accounting fraud ultimately was uncovered.

Bad signs that are *visible* are the best indicators of bad signs that are *invisible*. A dirty kitchen, says Buffett, rarely has just one cockroach. Seeing one is enough to tell you that there are more lurking in the walls. If you think they're there, they probably *are* there.

Enron exhibited many of these warning signs—Enron's management fleeced millions of shareholders—so scrutinize the quality of management to avoid the damage incompetent, unethical, and greedy leadership can incur.

To avoid these kinds of disasters and to increase your chances of a successful investment, always do the following:

Assess the management team before you invest. The quality of management is almost as important as the quality of the underlying business. Buffett only does business with ethical people whom he likes. He never profited from a company with unethical management.

Look for shareholder-friendly companies. Invest in companies with management that puts the needs of shareholders above its own needs. Look for companies that implement stock-repurchase plans to benefit shareholders and companies with a track record of frugality and rational allocation of capital.

Avoid investing in any company that has a record of financial or accounting shenanigans. Weak accounting usually means that management is trying to hide weak business performance.

If management stresses the *appearance* of performance over the *substance* of performance, says Buffett, keep your wallet in your pocket.

CHAPTER 15

☑ Remember, The Emperor Wears No Clothes on Wall Street

Wall Street, says Warren Buffett, is the only place where people go to in Rolls Royces to get advice from people who take the subway.

If you were to take a "conceptual walk" down Wall Street—in other words, taking notes on the various ideas you came across—you would find that there is no shortage of stock-picking schemes to choose from. You might even think that they were more or less impressive-sounding: technical analysis, market timing, intraday trading, wave theories, detrending oscillators, and so on. All are examples of touted methods that promise investors how to decipher the stock market and—ostensibly—succeed as an investor.

Where do all these techniques come from? Mainly from two sources: academics and financial professionals, almost all of whom have impressive credentials. And the concepts seem to have some merit, at least on first glance. Take "technical analysis," for example. People who engage in this arcane craft focus almost exclusively on market data. They look at price movements, trading volume, and the shape of charts showing stock-price performance—on the theory (1) that market prices represent the sum of all that needs to be known about a given stock and (2) that an individual can't come close to beating that collective wisdom.

A good theory? Not if you're in the Buffett camp! A technical analyst once summarized the stock market's one-day performance as follows: "It was a bonus day for traders as the major indices had a trend-down air pocket following the basic First Hour strategy Flip Top pattern. . . . the rising prices on declining volume into month end and the artificial price action on Monday with the increased terror warning made the indices vulnerable to an air pocket. NYSE volume was only 1.4 billion. . . . the .50 retracement between the 45.78 bull market high and [the] 17.32 10/02 low is 31.55 and price has now formed a 17-day trading range at this retracement zone."

Did you follow that? If not, don't feel too bad. Do you think that the world's greatest investor, Warren Buffett, pays any attention to such gobbledygook? Absolutely not.

As a potential investor, you will be perpetually bombarded by various investment strategies based on charts, volume, and price movements. You will be deluged with opportunities to create instant wealth. Turn your TV on at 3 A.M. to hear them.

For example, consider these following enticing offers: "Discover a stock trading system which produces double-digit profits on almost every trade! Trade right off of Stock Market charts"; "Revolutionary new system . . . pays off from 34 to 45 percent Returns in Just One Week"; and so on and so on.

Fortunately, one man has stepped forward and stated what should be obvious: *The emperor has no clothes.* Warren Buffett considers investment analyses based solely on charts, volume, and price movements to be nothing more than balderdash and twaddle.

At the risk of stating the obvious, technical analysis runs almost *exactly contrary* to Buffett's own conceptual framework for investing. Technical analysis stands for focusing on volume, charts, and price movements in selecting stocks. Buffett stands for focusing on the *value of a business*.

Of course, advocates of technical analysis would be quick to cite examples proving the power of their model. And, of course, there are surely isolated cases in which investors have made big money quickly through technical analysis. But I know of no technical analysis practitioner who is worth $44 billion. So who are you going to believe?

I encourage prospective investors interested in long-term investment success to read Warren Buffett's article, "The Superinvestors of Graham and Doddsville," featured

in Ben Graham's book, *The Intelligent Investor*. This article discusses the success of a group of value investors
who studied under Benjamin Graham and David Dodd
and who have consistently outperformed the Standard &
Poor's (S&P) 500 Stock Index year in and year out.

Those investors, reports Buffett, seek out discrepancies between (1) the value of a business and (2) the price
of small pieces of that business in the market. It is almost
the exact opposite of technical analysis, with its obses-
sive concentration on models, patterns, data, and so on.
Intelligent investors, emphasizes Buffett, are value-orient-
ed investors.

Value investing is not sexy. It is not glamorous or
even particularly challenging from a purely intellectual
standpoint. In fact, it tends to be slow, plodding, and even
a little boring—the tortoise rather than the hare. As
such, it provides none of the excitement that active
traders so relish. And it makes no guarantees of success,
as the "chartists" are wont to do.

But the results achieved by Buffett and the other
Graham and Dodd investors speak for themselves. Value
investing provides a proven intellectual framework for
the investor. Simply stated, investing like Buffett requires
that you ignore things that make no sense. Ignore the
kinds of complicated, faddish investment strategies that
tell you little or nothing about the underlying business.

Here are three things you can do to help you
to understand what is truly important when it comes
to making investment decisions:

Ignore the charts. A value investor is not concerned with charts. Buffett makes a strong case for not looking at stock charts when making investment decisions. Ignore chartists who claim to be successful stock pickers based on volume and price history.

If someone tells you they have a "foolproof" method to get rich in the stock market, run, don't walk, for the nearest exit. Remember, the key to investing is patience and discipline.

Invest like Benjamin Graham. Graham told investors to "search for discrepancies between the value of a business and the price of small pieces of that business in the market." This is the key to value investing, and it's far more productive than getting dizzy studying hundreds of stock charts.

The prospectuses of most mutual funds say—in small print—that past performance is no guarantee of future success. Buffett says the same thing about the market: If history revealed the path to riches, librarians would be rich.

CHAPTER 16

☑ **Practice Independent Thinking**

When investing, you need to *think independently*.

Independent thinking is one of Warren Buffett's greatest strengths, and he recommends it to the rest of us. This may sound like a bit of a truism: Of *course* you should think independently, right? But, in fact, many of us engage in what might be called "dependent thinking," in which our opinions are shaped mainly by what *others* think. This isn't independent thinking; in fact, it's more like mindless imitation.

Because he has achieved quasi-celebrity status, Buffett gets a lot of scrutiny—and, by extension, a lot of praise and criticism in response to his investment decisions. But Buffett does not depend on the validation of others in making those decisions. He is immune to their applause when they praise him, and he is quite comfortable ignoring them when they condemn him.

Buffett learned a very important lesson from Ben Graham: "You're neither right nor wrong because people agree with you. You're right because your facts and your reasoning are right." Whether many people or important people agree or disagree with you doesn't make you right or wrong; good thinking informed by good facts makes you right. This is the heart of independent thinking—using facts and reasoning to reach a conclusion and then *sticking* to that conclusion regardless of whether or not people agree with you.

A look back at the recent Internet bubble shows the value of independent thinking and illustrates how thinking based on facts and reasoning is far superior to that based on prevailing public opinion. The great bubble was an amazing period in recent stock market history. During those heady times, the birth of an exciting new industry (and spin-off industries) spawned hundreds of companies and created thousands of new millionaires.

One of the more remarkable things about those new Internet and high-tech companies, of course, was the meteoric rise in their stock prices and capitalization. Some Internet companies only a year or two old were worth more than much more established Fortune 500 companies. For example, EToys.com hit $86 a share and had a $10 billion capitalization. Webvan.com's peak capitalization was $7.5 billion.

Needless to say, millions of investors were enjoying tremendous gains through their high-tech holdings. People were getting rich—and getting rich quick. Ironically,

Berkshire Hathaway was not doing well during that same period, and its share price reflected it. Despite the tremendous gains made by high-tech stocks, Buffett refused to buy a single Internet stock or participate in this new "gold rush" in any way.

> **Stay away from a *rampaging* herd. If you don't, you and your investments might get stampeded.**

Consequently, Buffett bore the brunt of a lot of disparagement. He was ridiculed by pundits and criticized by shareholders. The media had a field day questioning Buffett's abilities. The financial weekly *Barron's* wrote on December 27, 1999, in its headline: "Warren, What's Wrong? Warren Buffett, America's Most Renowned Investor, Stumbled Badly This Year. Will His Berkshire Hathaway Recover?"

Other publications had the following headlines: "A Three Decade Legend Loses Some Luster," "Is Buffett Washed Up?" and "Tech Phobia May Topple Buffett." Many people felt that Buffett should invest in high-tech stocks, and they could not understand how he could pass up such opportunities. But despite the public censure—even ridicule—he stuck to his guns and didn't budge.

Buffett's facts and reasoning were clear: He did not understand these Internet businesses and therefore stayed away from them. He had no idea which one of these high-tech companies would have a long-term competitive advantage and how they would be performing in 10 years.

He also believed that irrational market psychology was responsible for many of the high-tech share prices. In such a circumstance, he believes, stock prices are actually set by the people who are greediest, or most emotional, or most depressed—in other words, by people who are detached from long-term reality. The result can be stock prices that are "nonsensical."

Based on this thinking, Buffett decided not to invest in any of these companies, even as millions of investors fell all over themselves to buy their high-flying stocks. Buffett felt that he was right because his facts and reasoning were right; he did not feel that he was wrong simply because almost everyone disagreed with him. His independent thinking was later vindicated when the great bubble burst and high-tech stocks collapsed.

As a result, most Internet companies went bankrupt, and the tech-heavy Nasdaq experienced more than a 75 percent decrease in value. Hundreds of billions of stock market dollars went up in smoke. What would have happened if Buffett had followed public opinion and joined the Internet herd? Mindless imitation of others would have cost him dearly.

Based on experiences such as this, some investors conclude that a contrarian investing strategy is superior to a "follow-the-crowd strategy." ("Contrarians," as the name implies, simply run in the *other* direction from the herd.) But again, Buffett disagrees. If the herd is doing the wrong thing, going 180 degrees in the opposite direction may be no better. This is investing based on *polling* rather than thinking, says Buffett—and any investment strategy based on polling rather than thinking has to be a bad strategy.

It's all about *thinking*—clearly and independently. And the stakes are high. Buffett is fond of quoting philosopher Bertrand Russell: "Most men would rather die than think. Many do."

The lesson to be learned from Buffett is to rely on *facts* and *reasoning* in making your investment decisions. Do not make a decision just because it is the popular or contrarian thing to do.

Never substitute popular wisdom for independent thinking. Don't follow the herd. Do your homework and make your own investment choices. Do not allow yourself to be taken in by others or make a decision just because it is the "in thing" to do.

Make independent thinking one of your portfolio's greatest assets. Being smart isn't good enough, says Buffett. Lots of high-IQ people fall victim to the herd mentality. Independent thinking is one of Buffett's greatest strengths. Make it one of your own.

Do not be a mindless contrarian investor. Buffett believes that doing *anything* mindlessly is the wrong thing to do. Don't follow the herd mindlessly and don't go against it mindlessly in the spirit of contrarianism. Both paths lead to dangerous places.

Gather your facts, sit down, and *think*, advises Buffett. There is no substitute!

CHAPTER 17

☑ Stay within Your Circle of Competence

Develop a zone of expertise, operate within that zone, and don't beat yourself up for missing opportunities that arise *outside* that zone.

When it comes to picking which businesses to invest in, Warren Buffett is guided by what he calls his "circle of competence." His circle of competence includes only those stocks and industries in which he feels most comfortable to be involved in.

As noted previously, Buffett did not invest in high-tech companies during the high-tech boom. Why? Because they were outside his circle of competence. And *lots* of industries, stresses Buffett, fall outside that circle. He and his associate, Charlie Munger, don't consider themselves experts in computer-chip technology, in the assessment of commodity futures, or in the potential of mineral prospects. *It's not what they do.*

They don't think of themselves as being skilled at dealing with fast-moving companies or industries. In his public utterances, Buffett grants that there may well be people out there who have acquired some sort of predictive skill that helps decode the long-term prospects of companies in the fast lane—but he knows that *he* doesn't possess that skill. And lacking it, he says, he simply has to stick with what he knows.

Buffett is intensely disciplined about his circle of competence. He makes *no investments outside that circle*—period. And he resists the temptation to make the circle bigger. In fact, he says, the size of your circle of competence is not particularly important. What is important is knowing where the boundaries are and staying within them. Drift outside that circle, and the chances of making investment mistakes grow exponentially. See something outside your circle—something new and exciting—toward which the herd is stampeding? *Stay away.*

Every year (since 1982) Buffett lists a "businesses wanted" ad in his annual reports, advertising for the types of businesses he would like to buy. He seeks

1. Large purchases (at least $50 million of before-tax earnings)

2. Businesses that have demonstrated consistent earnings power (rosy projections of future earnings are of no interest)

3. Businesses earning good returns on equity while carrying little or no debt

4. Businesses with strong management in place

5. Simple businesses (read: "not a lot of complex technology")

6. An offering price (a company with no visible price tag is likely to waste Buffett's time)

This ad is of particular interest in this discussion because it specifically outlines Buffett's circle of competence—the business arena where he is most comfortable making investment decisions. This is, in effect, his checklist for determining if an investment is inside his circle.

Although Buffett might not understand microchips, nanotechnology, and gigabytes, he does understand cowboy boots, bricks, carpet, and paint. A look back at the year 2000 shows Buffett at work in his circle. He bought both Justin Industries, a leading maker of cowboy boots, and Acme, a Texas brick manufacturer.

Bricks? How interesting can bricks be? Interesting enough, Buffett replies, if it's the right company. When asked to name a brand of brick, Buffett continues, three out of four Texans say, "Acme." The company cranks out a *billion* bricks a year, or close to 12 percent of all bricks produced in the United States annually. In the same year that he bought Acme, Buffett also purchased (for $1 billion in cash) the Benjamin Moore Paint Company, which has been making paint for 117 years. And finally, he also bought 87 percent of the world's largest carpet manu-facturer, Shaw Industries.

Boots, bricks, carpet, and paint—they may not sound exciting, but their earnings capability is very exciting. Three years after being purchased by Buffett, Acme Brick, Benjamin Moore Paint, and Shaw Industries all reported record earnings. The lesson? Stay within your circle of competence. Act on what you *know*. If you do, you're better able to act *fast* and more likely to act *big*. By steadfastly sticking to this principle, Buffett has increased Berkshire Hathaway's book value from $19.46 per share in 1965 to more than $50,000 in 2005. No other investor comes close to such an accomplishment.

As an investor, you need to specifically define for yourself a circle of competence. By extension, you also need to define what is *outside* your circle of compe-tence. Initial public offerings (IPOs), shorting stocks, mutual funds, futures, penny stocks, and options—do you understand these things? Can you evaluate their future profitability successfully? If you cannot understand or evaluate them, then they are outside your circle of com-petence, and you should not get involved with them.

Charlie Munger likes to use the mental model of three baskets on your desk: "In," "Out," and "Too tough." Munger says that he and Buffett put a large percentage of all the investment opportunities that come their way into the "Too tough" basket.

The takeaway: Create a checklist just like Buffett does and invest only when those conditions are met.

Don't venture out of your circle. Put most things in the "Too tough" basket, act only when you feel competent in your analysis, and don't hesitate to act forcefully inside your area of competence.

Here are three rules to live by when putting together your investment portfolio:

Write down the industries and businesses with which you feel most comfortable. This will help you to define your circle of competence. If Buffett does not venture outside his circle, then you should not either.

Do not make exceptions to your circle-of-competence rule. Before making that one exception to your circle-of-competence rule, sit back and think: Why risk your money on things you don't understand or can't evaluate? Be disciplined enough not to make exceptions to the competency rule.

Play your game, not someone else's. The example that Buffett cites as an illustration is soybean futures. If someone else cleans up in the soybean market, says Buffett, fine—it's not his game. Stick to your own game.

If you can rule out 90 percent of the businesses in the United States as outside your circle of competence, you're likely to do a far better job investing in the remaining 10 percent.

CHAPTER 18

☑ Ignore Stock Market Forecasts

Short-term forecasts of stock or bond prices are useless, says Warren Buffett. They tell you more about the forecaster than they tell you about the future.

Ben Graham, Buffett's favorite writer about investing, once observed with puzzlement that so many investment professionals—stock brokers, investment counselors, financial advisors, and the like—seemed to place so much emphasis on market forecasts. Warren Buffett shares that puzzlement—which he extends to an active disdain. He compares short-term market forecasts to "poison" and suggests that they should be kept away from people who approach the market like children.

Buffett prefers to focus narrowly on the *performance of the business* and not to be distracted by larger trends that he believes are impossible to forecast with any accuracy. If he comes across an article that purports to look into the future—even by a distinguished economist in a reputable publication—he skips it. Why waste time on soothsaying, he asks rhetorically? That's time that could be spent on analyzing a *business*.

Charlie Munger likens the obsession with market forecasts to long-ago techniques for fortune-telling. Kings, he points out, used to hire people to interpret the entrails of slaughtered sheep. Today's forecasters, he asserts, are no better than wizards "reading" sheep guts.

As noted earlier, Buffett prefers to spend his time looking at things he has a good chance of figuring out. A business within his circle of competence may lend itself to being figured out. The stock markets are a "mystery" to Buffett—and they're not a mystery that anyone is likely to figure out. Yes, there's always another forecast coming down the pipe, often with a respectable name attached to it. No matter: A key part of Buffett's success is his ability to tune out such forecasts as distractions.

Distractions can only inhibit action and cloud one's judgment. Why? In part, because they create an *illusion of precision*. They *seem* to be data-driven, and their analyses *seem* to grow directly out of the data. All untrue, says Buffett; in fact, the more precise a forecast seems to be, the more skeptical *you* should be. Again, the point is to look at proven performance rather than at projections and predictions. Don't let prognostications pull your eye off the ball; stay focused on what's actually important. Stay at the *company* level rather than the market level; spend your time analyzing a company's past and present performance to gain a better idea of its future. Look for that promising opportunity without letting forecasts get in the way of your decisions.

Buffett purchased National Indemnity in 1967, See's Candies in 1972, the *Buffalo News* in 1977, the Nebraska Furniture Mart in 1983, and Scott Fetzer in 1986. Why those years? Because that's when they became available. Why those companies? Because they were available, because they survived Buffett's careful scrutiny, and because the price was right. How much did larger trends—the strength of the national economy, the direction of the Dow, the public mutterings of the Fed chairman—enter into those calculations? If you take Buffett at his word—and there's no reason not to—the answer is: *Not at all*. Predictions about the future simply were not part of the equation when he made his decision whether to invest or not.

Some investors feel that forecasts make the future clear—and that the next forecast is the one that's going to make everything clear. Nonsense, says Buffett; the future is always obscure. Waiting for the future to come clear—whether through the use of market forecasts or other purported tools—could mean waiting forever. Don't wait for certainty, advises Buffett; investing is all about *acting* once you've spotted a good business blessed with good management. Don't get paralyzed by the fortune-tellers. Spot the target and pull the trigger.

And *don't get emotional.* Forecasts may seem like the opposite of emotion, drenched as they are in facts and figures. But putting your faith in those facts and figures is 100 percent an emotional act. Stay in the realm of the observable. Don't make guesses; make informed judgments.

To summarize, here are three tips on how to handle forecasts the Buffett way:

Eliminate forecasts from any involvement in your investment decisions. Buffett doesn't pay attention to short-term stock market forecasts; neither should you.

Take the time you would spend listening to forecasts and instead use it to analyze a business's track record. We all would like to know what the future holds, but we can't. No one has a crystal ball; the future is never certain. Concentrate on what is known and don't worry about the unknown.

Develop an investing strategy that does not depend on the overall movement of the market. Remember, Warren Buffett—the world's greatest investor—confesses that he can't *begin* to predict the movement of the markets. Most likely neither can you. Concentrate on putting together a portfolio characterized by solid businesses that are likely to succeed regardless of whether the market goes up or down.

The more volatile or more speculative the markets, the more likely that people will begin to turn to forecasts for help—but this is when forecasts have the *least* chance of being right. The more precise someone claims to be in a volatile market, the more skeptical *you* should be.

CHAPTER 19

✔ Understand "Mr. Market" and the "Margin of Safety"

What makes for a good investor? According to Warren Buffett, a good investor is someone who combines good business judgment with an ability to ignore the wild swings of the marketplace. When the emotions start to swirl, says Buffett, remember Ben Graham's "Mr. Market" concept, and look for a "margin of safety."

W arren Buffett studied under Benjamin Graham at Columbia University. Buffett was, incidentally, the only student in Graham's 22 years of teaching to get an A+ from Graham. Graham taught Buffett two very important concepts that he still follows today. One is the

"Mr. Market" allegory, and the second is to always have a margin of safety with the purchase price.

These two ideas, along with viewing stocks as part ownership of a business, are the Graham "Rocks of Gibraltar." Buffett feels that if an investor has a grasp of these three basic ideas, he will put himself in a position to do well. Buffett alluded to these concepts on the one-hundredth anniversary of Graham's birth, saying that they were valid then and were likely to be important a century into the future.

Who, or what, is the "Mr. Market" invented all those years ago by Buffett's mentor Ben Graham?

Buffett describes Mr. Market as a business partner—one with incurable emotional problems who appears every day, without fail, and names a price at which he will either buy or sell you his interest in the business.

Mr. Market, according to Buffett, is what used to be called "manic-depressive" and today might be called "bipolar." His psychological troubles intrude on the prices he quotes. When he's feeling euphoric, he sees only good things in the business and puts a high price on his holdings. In truth, when he's in this mood, he doesn't really want to sell you his interest because he's afraid you'll accept his price, buy his shares, and get the benefit of all the price appreciation that he thinks is just around the corner.

And then there's the *dark* side of Mr. Market. When he's down, he sees nothing but trouble, inside and outside the business. In this mood, he's afraid you'll unload your holdings on *him*, and he'll be left holding the bag during the coming downward spiral. In this mood, he puts a low asking price on his shares and hopes that you'll grab them.

Mr. Market is nothing if not persistent, explains Buffett. He comes around every day, no matter what mood he's in. He doesn't seem to mind if you ignore him; he'll be back tomorrow with a quote. All you have to do is figure out what mood Mr. Market is in and decide what you're going to do about it. Ignore him? Take advantage of him? Again, he doesn't seem to mind which way you go.

But the key, says Buffett—paraphrasing Graham—is *never to fall under his influence.* That influence can be powerful at times. His gloom can fill the room. His euphoria can be intoxicating. *Read the mood,* says Buffett, *and act in ways that take the mood into account—but don't get swept up in the mood yourself.*

Ben Graham's "Mr. Market" is a metaphor that every value investor should use as the basis for understanding the price workings of the stock market. It helps to make sense of market madness. And it helps to signal and underscore the arrival of opportunity. As an investor, you always should be ready to exploit Mr. Market when he is depressed and share prices are falling. This means that good businesses are getting tarred by a bigger brush. This is exactly the time for aggressive opportunism—for seizing of an opportunity that is presented by stock market silliness and for making a big investment in a stock because you believe its intrinsic value is higher than its price.

When the stock market crash of 1987 pushed down the price of Coca-Cola, Buffett took advantage of "Mr. Market's" gloom, which was then imposing an unnaturally low price on a business that Buffett knew to be solid. He bought $1 billion worth of Coca-Cola stock at an average price of about $11 a share. He felt that Coca-Cola was a great franchise and that at the time the intrinsic value of Coca-Cola was greater than its low stock price. It was, he later explained, the most powerful brand in the world. Its products are relatively cheap and are universally liked. Per capita consumption tends to go up year after year in countries around the world. Mr. Market is down on this stock? Excellent, says Buffett; time to buy. It's like the department store that is going out of business, and everything is marked down 50 percent: This is a great opportunity to buy things of value at a great price.

After adding Mr. Market to your intellectual framework, you also need to grasp the importance of *margin of safety*—another of Ben Graham's principles. Simply put, "margin of safety" means that the price of the stock is *substantially* lower than the value of the business. You don't want the price and value of the business to be close. You want a lot of daylight between those two figures—an "enormous margin," in Buffett's words.

Once again, you want to buy the dollar bill that is selling for 40 cents on the stock market. Buffett talks about driving a 10,000-pound truck across a bridge designed to carry 30,000 pounds—in other words, plenty of room for error.

And here's where the irrationality of Mr. Market works in your favor. Eventually, he gets *very* gloomy, causing share prices to fall precipitously. This gives you an opportunity to achieve a margin of safety in the purchase of shares. Eventually, says Buffett, the market will recognize their value, and their price will rise. *Sooner or later,* Buffett says confidently, *value counts.*

Again, don't let Mr. Market suck you into his mood. Don't let him value businesses for you, emphasizes Buffett. He is your *servant* rather than your guide.

When assessing the margin of safety, says Buffett, use the concept of "intrinsic value" as your starting point. This is the measurement that really counts. It attempts to determine the discounted value of the cash that can be taken out of the business during its remaining life.

It is, as Buffett is the first to admit, a "highly subjective" estimate. Future cash flows get revised up or down, and intrinsic value floats along with them. The variability of interest rates also affects any calculation of intrinsic value. Nevertheless, says Buffett, it remains the most useful starting point for understanding the relative attractiveness of an investment compared with an alternative investment.

This is yet another reason why Buffett prefers easy-to-understand businesses: He can look at their earnings, cash flow, and capital needed to run their companies, and he can use that information to analyze their intrinsic value. He then can see if there is a significant discrepancy between price and value.

Your goal? To do what Buffett does and to take advantage of mistakes by Mr. Market when he attaches low prices to businesses that are worth a lot more. When Mr. Market's gloom creates a margin of safety, it's time to act.

Make sure that you understand Buffett's concepts of Mr. Market and the margin of safety. This will help you to attain the proper mind-set to make better investment decisions.

Heed Buffett's analogies. Buffett has commented that like the Lord, the market helps those who help themselves. But—he is quick to add—the market doesn't forgive those who "know not what they do."

Bide your time, and wait for Mr. Market to get depressed and lower stock prices enough to provide a margin-of-safety buying opportunity. Once again, Buffett's advice of patience and discipline come through loud and clear. If you can develop his level of discipline and wait for an opportunity, you will be rewarded.

Some people complain about market volatility. Not Buffett: He believes that volatility—Mr. Market's dramatic mood swings—is what creates opportunity for savvy investors. Wait until other people start acting foolishly, and then act wisely.

CHAPTER 20

☑ Be Fearful When Others Are Greedy and Greedy When Others Are Fearful

You can safely predict that people will be greedy, fearful, or foolish, says Buffett. You just can't predict when or in what order.

The stock market always will be influenced by periodic epidemics of the powerful emotions of greed and fear. "I can calculate the motions of the heavenly bodies but not the madness of people," Isaac Newton once said. Warren Buffett often exploits outbreaks of these highly contagious emotions by behaving in a way opposite to the prevailing sentiment.

If most investors are greedy, then Buffett becomes "fearful" (or at least extremely conservative). If most investors are fearful, Buffett gets "greedy" (or at least unusually acquisitive). By following this strategy, Buffett has made a lot of money while others were not so successful.

In the 1960s, the stock market embarked on a sleigh ride in which prices shot up and volume soared. A lot of people got very excited about the stock market—and in the process contributed heavily to driving up share prices. In other words, as the balloon started to fill up, people eagerly pumped more hot air into it. It is in this phase of the moon—the phase of overheated avarice—that Buffett almost always chooses to sit on the sidelines.

He will not make investments while stock prices are rising irrationally and are decoupled from the actual value of the underlying business—in other words, situations in which prices have escaped the gravitational pull of actual business performance.

Eventually, predictably, this bull market of the 1960s came crashing to its end. And when the stock market collapsed, the great herd of investors became very fearful, as they almost always do after an irrational euphoric period. Instead of buying stocks, people dumped their shares, thereby driving prices down. They simply stopped investing.

The early 1970s were a notorious bear market. People were selling their shares out of fear. In

1973-1974, the economy was in recession, things were gloomy, and the Dow Jones had plunged below 700. Having gotten this far in this book, you probably can predict what *else* happened in this period: Buffett started buying. In fact, he started buying *a lot*. It was at this time, for example, that he made his now legendary *Washington Post* investment.

Unfortunately, as Buffett has observed, the irrational mood swings—from euphoria to misery and back again—aren't limited to naive investors. Professionals, including pension fund managers, are equally susceptible. At the market peak in 1971, Buffett points out, pension funds were committing all their available funds to the equity markets. A scant three years later, after the bottom had fallen out, they were investing only one dollar in five in equities. They got it *exactly wrong*, concludes Buffett—getting intoxicated when others were getting intoxicated and getting scared when others were getting scared. They did not take advantage of low prices but instead bought shares at high prices and then sold them when prices dropped.

Buffett, of course, behaved far differently. He made a large number of investments when the stock market was offering great companies at rock-bottom prices. He took advantage of the discounted shares of good businesses.

We also know how Buffett became very fearful during the Internet stock bull market when everyone else was buying shares greedily. He did not lose any money, while millions of Americans ended up losing their shirts on Internet stocks. Periods of fear and greed will break out intermittently and grip the investment community. You must behave exactly as Buffett does in these situations and use these emotions to your advantage.

Here are rules to live by when formulating your "fearful when people are greedy" investment strategy:

Buy when people are selling and sell when people are buying. Program yourself to be fearful when most investors are greedy. Stocks are most interesting, says Buffett, when almost nobody is interested in them. This is true of many markets—commercial real estate being another good example—but it's especially striking in the stock markets, where the stampeding of the herd is so easy to detect. (In fact, given the pervasiveness of financial news coverage today, it's impossible to overlook the herd.) When people in the herd are fearful, they are not interested in buying stocks—but that's exactly when you *should* be interested. Of course, follow the other piece of Buffett's advice and do not invest blindly or mindlessly. Only when the investment in question meets your selection criteria should you make the investment.

Be ready to act quickly when opportunity strikes. When the Dow Jones Industrial Average hit rock bottom in 1974 at 580, Buffett likened himself to an "oversexed guy in a whorehouse." Be ready to act quickly and courageously when fear prevails and market prices plummet.

What will happen tomorrow? Will the market go up, down, or sideways? To Warren Buffett, these are uninteresting questions—except insofar as the "contagious diseases" of fear and greed will affect his own investing prospects, either by driving down prices and creating opportunities (fear) or by driving up prices and closing off opportunities (greed). When opportunities arise, Buffett is prepared to move. When greed prevails, Buffett is prepared to wait on the sidelines.

CHAPTER 21

☑ Read, Read Some More, and Then Think

How does Warren Buffett—the world's greatest investor—spend his time? By his own reckoning, he spends something like six hours a day reading and an hour or two on the phone. The rest of the time, he *thinks*.

Warren Buffett, like most great thinkers, is a voracious reader. He reads the *Financial Times*, the *Wall Street Journal*, the *New York Times*, and financial magazines such as *Fortune*. Some of this is just general background reading, but a lot of it is focused on a particular prospect. When a company gets into Buffett's crosshairs, he begins reading everything he can about that company and its industry.

In particular, he is constantly reading annual reports. When Buffett is interested in a company, he will buy some shares of its *competitors* just so he can get their annual reports. Again, it's far-ranging reading, but it's also reading for a purpose. Extensive reading arms Buffett with the facts and ideas that fuel his independent thinking and reasoning. It's not an exaggeration to say that Buffett's reading—combined with his thinking, of course—has been the foundation of his achievements.

Buffett recommends that everyone read his favorite book on investing, Ben Graham's book, *The Intelligent Investor,* because of the intellectual framework it provides. He recommends special attention to Chapter 8 ("Market Fluctuations") and Chapter 20 ("Margin of Safety"). Phil Fisher's book, *Common Stocks and Uncommon Profits,* is worth reading. And no library would be complete without Graham and Dodd's *Security Analysis,* first published in 1934 (in the interest of full disclosure, that book also was published by McGraw-Hill).

A value investor should read everything he can about Warren Buffett and Charlie Munger. On the BerkshireHathaway.com Web site, available for all to read, is every one of Buffett's letters to shareholders and annual reports since 1977. They are an absolute gold mine of information and wisdom for every potential investor and are a must-read.

So the first rule is to *read, read, and read some more*. But the second rule is to *read selectively*. By now, you should have a sense of the kinds of reading materials that are useful to a value investor—and conversely, those that are completely useless. There are only so many hours in the day and only so many reading hours before your eyes get tired. Don't waste those valuable hours on market forecasts, prognostications, and formula-heavy theories.

For example? One theory of which Buffett is particularly scornful is the "efficient market theory" (EMT). Often propounded by professors at leading business schools, EMT asserts that the markets are completely efficient. In other words, every share is priced exactly where it should be because all the pushes and pulls of the marketplace have led to that state of grace and wisdom. If this is true, then analyzing businesses is a waste of time because you will either wind up at the "right" valuation—the market valuation—or you will wind up at some other valuation that is, by definition, wrong.

Buffett watched with amazement as this theory gradually made its way out of academia and into the marketplace. Once the hobbyhorse of only a few high-profile finance professors, EMT soon became the mantra of investment professionals and corporate executives alike. *Share prices reflect all public information about a stock,* they proclaimed, more or less in unison, *so there's no need to dig any deeper.*

Offensive as EMT was to someone like Buffett, it was also a source of enormous competitive advantage. Stock picking is an *intellectual* enterprise, says Buffett, much like chess or bridge. It's a great luxury, Buffett points out, to sit down across the chess board from someone who doesn't believe in thinking while playing.

This may sound like a tempest in an intellectual teapot, but it isn't. In 1973, many institutional investors were strong adherents of EMT. Accordingly, few were interested in buying shares in the Washington Post Company, which were then to be had at rock-bottom prices. The company's shares, said EMT devotees, were exactly where they deserved to be and weren't worth buying. Buffett—ever mindful of his training at the knee of Ben Graham—snapped them up and soon proved the EMT devotees wrong.

In retrospect, the gulf between market valuation and intrinsic value is easy to see. At that time, the market was valuing the Washington Post Company at around $100 million. Buffett saw an intrinsic value of between $400 and $500 million—and began buying heavily.

The lesson? While other thinkers were reading about EMT, Buffett was reading Graham—and, of course, reading everything he could get his hands on about the *Washington Post* Company and its industry—and the results speak for themselves. Read constantly, but read things that will inform—rather than distort—your investment worldview. Don't worry about the latest intellectual fad that is escaping from the business schools into a gullible marketplace. (Remember the herd!) Worry about finding value, which in many cases begins with good reading habits.

Get in the habit of reading. Buffett and Munger are avid readers, and they learn mostly from books, periodicals, annual reports, 10-Ks, 10-Qs, and other specialized publications. *Increase your reading to feed your thinking.*

Read Buffett's annual reports and letters. It's hard to overstate this point. The acknowledged master in the world of investing has posted his thinking on the Web for all to see. You aim to emulate his success—so shouldn't you start there? The specifics are valuable, of course. But even more valuable is the opportunity to see *how his mind works* in a relatively unvarnished way. Study Buffett's annual reports and letters to acquire good habits of mind.

Restrict your time only to things worth reading. Read Buffett and Graham but don't read nonsense. Avoid anything to do with EMT or similar "disciplines." They will only distract you from the real task at hand.

Buffett believes that—unlike some other industries—the investment industry is one in which knowledge accumulates and is there to be uncovered by those who are willing to do some digging. His advice: *Be a digger.* In most cases, this translates directly into *Be a reader.*

CHAPTER 22

☑ Use All Your Horsepower

How big is your engine, and how efficiently do you put it to work? Warren Buffett suggests that lots of people have "400-horsepower engines" but only 100 horsepower of output. (Smart people, in other words, often allow themselves to get distracted from the task at hand and act in irrational ways.) The person who gets full output from a 200-horsepower engine, says Buffett, is a lot better off.

Warren Buffett is a big believer in the importance of good habits. Habits effectively determine behavior, and good habits lead to good behaviors.

Buffett suggests that people should conduct an exercise to check the efficacy—the "output"—of their own habits and behaviors. Write down the qualities of a person you greatly admire, advises Buffett, and then make a list of the qualities of a person you don't admire at all. (Don't use yourself as one of the two examples in this exercise.) Study the two lists. How are they different? Are they different only in the specifics, or can you see any patterns?

Next, says Buffett, try to adopt the qualities of the person you admire most. Why? Because if these habits are practiced regularly, they can become *your* habits. At the same time, stop acting out all the negative qualities of the person you *don't* admire. If you stick to it, your behaviors will change. If you look back 20 years from now, says Buffett, you'll be acting out all those good habits and their associated behaviors, and you'll be acting out none of the bad ones.

Develop positive habits. Eschew and expunge your bad ones. The result, according to Buffett? A more direct correlation between your horsepower and your output.

For your positive role model, you could do far worse than emulating Buffett himself. His father imbued in him the highest standards of integrity and ethics. Under Buffett, Berkshire Hathaway pays billions of dollars in annual taxes to the U.S. government and does not have a single overseas tax shelter. In contrast, Enron created 881 offshore subsidiaries, 692 of them in the Cayman Islands, in order to avoid paying taxes. Buffett has proven that great behavior can be consistent with great profits. The Enrons, Adelphias, and Tycos of the world remind us how quickly dishonest and unethical conduct can lead to financial catastrophe.

A great deal has been written about Buffett, so it would not be difficult to develop a longer list of habits and behaviors that you might want to emulate. (And don't forget to sketch out the complementary portrait— of that person you'd *never* want to emulate!) But no matter who you decide to hold up as a role model, develop as long a list as possible of characteristics that you want to make your own.

Here are a few questions you might want to ask yourself to make sure that you are not sabotaging your own investment strategy:

1. Do you do sufficient homework and due diligence on companies before you buy them?

2. Do you check your stocks only periodically and avoid the "daily" noise and "talking heads"?

3. Do you ignore stock tips regardless of their source?

4. Do you avoid the herd and instead make your own investment decisions (based on independent thinking)?

5. Do you exhibit patience by waiting patiently for companies to grow in intrinsic value?

6. Do you avoid investing in companies, businesses, or industries that you don't understand?

7. Do you strike (i.e., buy) when people are frightened and sell when people are greedy?

8. Do you confine your investments to a select number of holdings, thereby not diluting your potential gains?

9. Do you live by the rules of Mr. Market and the margin of safety?

10. Do you read key financial newspapers and magazines on a consistent basis?

If you answered yes to eight or more of these questions, you may consider yourself a true Buffett believer and protégé. More important, of course, you are well on your way to building your own investment successes.

If you responded yes to between five and seven of these questions, not bad. You practice a good part of the Buffett doctrine, but you also have room for improvement.

If you responded yes to four or fewer of these questions, you have some work to do. But take heart. As Buffett says, you can put habits into effect now that you will have 20 years from now.

Make sure that you have the right role models. Show me a person's heroes, says Buffett, and I'll tell you what kind of person he is and where he's headed. So who are *your* heroes? Have you made their qualities your habits?

Strive for rational behavior, good habits, and proper temperament. Some experts contend that after only *21 days*, a repeated practice becomes a habit. Why not invest the three weeks and find out for yourself whether they're right? You have nothing to lose—except bad habits, of course—and everything to gain.

Write down the habits, practices, and philosophies that you want to make your own. Then be sure to keep track of them and—eventually—*own* them.

Financial success is a "matter of having the right habits."

CHAPTER 23

☑ **Avoid the Costly Mistakes of Others**

Buffett's friend and associate Charlie Munger always emphasizes the study of mistakes so as not to go there.

It is very important to study the mistakes of other investors so as not to "go there" yourself. Unfortunately, there is no greater source of mistakes than what recent retirees have done with their stock market portfolios.

In the late 1990s, one prospective retiree with $385,000 in his retirement account attended a retirement seminar. There he heard a presentation by a broker who urged the attendees to accept their company's early retirement buyout and then turn over their savings to him to invest in a portfolio of his own design.

The attendees were told that they would then live comfortably in retirement on the earnings and possibly become millionaires in a few years. The broker proceeded to invest this retiree's money into shares in technology, health care, financial services, and high-load mutual funds.

When the value of his portfolio dropped close to $100,000, this person had no other choice but to return to the workplace. For the time being, at least, all this person's hopes and dreams for a secure retirement went up in smoke.

Or consider the unfortunate retiree who invested her lifetime savings of $410,000 with a broker who told her that she would earn enough money in the stock market to withdraw $3,000 a month in retirement. This broker invested the bulk of this unfortunate woman's money in Internet stocks, technology stocks, and mutual funds. When he was "finished," the value of the woman's portfolio had plunged to a paltry $38,000.

Sadly, there are many hardworking Americans who find themselves in this place. There are thousands of terrible stories of hardworking people who spent 25 years of their lives working and saving for retirement only to see their savings disappear because of poor investment decisions.

Many of these retirees felt that they knew nothing about the stock market and were incapable of managing their own money and making investments. Better leave it to a "professional," they thought.

Enticed by the sales pitches of brokers and empty promises of wealth, they became victims of unsound investing—investing that was based on hyperactivity, high-fee investments with big commissions, timing the market, and shares in crummy companies.

All these tales occurred under the auspices of "professional money management."

The most important lesson to be learned from these stories is *the importance of sound investing.* A solid understanding of basic investing fundamentals—many of which have been presented throughout this book— offers the best protection against unsound financial schemes and enticements.

Most of us will, at one time or another, be tempted by sales pitches that promise untold amounts of wealth, formulas for unlocking the mysteries of the stock market, and invitations to invest in unproven companies. Consider the following "come-on": "Investing in this stock now could bring a windfall of profits. Imagine investing in ExxonMobil or one of the major energy companies in its infancy stage!"

See those wiggle words—"could" and "imagine"? You have to have learned enough—and be disciplined enough—to ignore these kinds of seductive sales pitches that play on your emotions (and carefully avoid making any real promises). You have to follow the fundamentals of sound value investing that are espoused and practiced by Warren Buffett. If you do, you'll give yourself a much better chance of seeing your investments grow and flourish rather than wither on the vine.

Charlie Munger says: "There are huge advantages for an individual to get into a position where you make a few great investments and just sit back. You're paying less to brokers. You're listening to less nonsense." Never forget that there will always be a lot of nonsense on Wall Street, so just pay attention to the things that make sense.

And finally, pay close attention to the *costs* associated with your investments. Today, literally hundreds of no-load or commission-free funds are available, and stock trading has become nearly a commodity service. So there is absolutely *no reason* to pay hefty commissions for a fund or a stock.

The hidden fees associated with many kinds of investments will kill your returns. Become a savvy investor by asking questions and watching costs.

The hidden fees and commissions associated with many kinds of investments rob investors of their ability to make money over the long run. Some funds, for example, charge up-front commissions of *more than 6 percent*. This means that if you purchase the fund, it must increase in value by 6 percent before you can break even, let alone start making money. Avoid these types of investments by opting for no-load funds.

Make sure that you don't fall in with the wrong kind of investment "advisor." Consider these steps to make sure that you do not fall prey to the types of schemes that do little more than separate investors from their money:

If it sounds too good to be true, it probably is. Be wary of promises of instant riches and high returns. They almost always come with huge amounts of risk. And just as bad, they almost always include pricey commissions for the person who sells you that "great investment."

Get actively involved in your own decision making and never abdicate control of your portfolio. Instead of listening to false prophets, make your own decisions based on your own risk tolerance levels. In doing so, observe the rules and principles highlighted throughout this book.

Always watch costs. Remember that people trying to sell you something do it because of the fat commissions they will reap on your hard-earned money. Always ask about costs, read prospectuses, and learn as much as you can about the costs associated with any investment. And if you are still paying more than $100 per stock market transaction, consider opening an online account with a discount broker (such as TD Waterhouse or E*TRADE). Since you will be making your own investment decisions, there is no need to pay high commissions to a broker.

Learn from the other guy's mistakes, says Buffett. There's no reason to live through an unhappy drama that someone else has already lived through.

CHAPTER 24

✓ Become a Sound Investor

Buffett says that Ben Graham was about "sound investing." He wasn't about brilliant investing or fads and fashions, and the good thing about sound investing is that it can make you wealthy if you are in not too much of a hurry, and it never makes you poor, which is even better.

Warren Buffett—through his words and actions—has laid out a proven path for investors to follow. By following Buffett's advice, the average investor can practice sound value investing and can achieve sound results without the services of a professional.

Let us review Buffett's fundamentals. He likes to keep things simple and easy. He avoids the complex and difficult. His ironclad rule is that he will invest only in things he understands, and he avoids everything else. He will do things only within his circle of competence.

He stays very disciplined when standing at the investment plate, and he only swings at pitches in his "sweet spot." He shuns hyperactivity and instead recommends long stretches of *inactivity*. He is quite comfortable with a grand total of 20 investment decisions in a lifetime. You often have to sit on your hands—that's just part of the game.

Buffett's investment style is not a get-rich-quick scheme. Instead, it's a get-rich-slow plan. It takes time for the acorn to become an oak tree.

Proper temperament is very important. Specifically, an investor must keep his head during the good times and the bad. He must hold on for dear life when he owns shares in a great business with a great management. An investor always must keep his eye on the business, its performance, its management, and its intrinsic value.

A stock is part of a business, and how the business performs ultimately will determine how the stock price performs. You want to buy shares in companies headed by competent and ethical managers who keep shareholders' interests paramount.

You do not want to overdiversify your holdings. Instead, you want to *concentrate* them in high-quality businesses.

There always will be great distractions for investors—endless significant macro events concerning geopolitics, changes in the economy, and a stream of never-ending stock market forecasts. To become a sound investor, you must ignore these distractions and focus on the underlying businesses. Ignore the ticker. Your concern is *value*, not price—unless, of course, a dip in price offers a new opportunity to invest where there is a margin of safety.

Mr. Market will help you to understand the stock market, and you will use the greed and fear of people to your advantage: You will be fearful when others are greedy and greedy when others are fearful.

You will realize that a lot of nonsense is practiced on Wall Street. For instance, some investors swear by streams of stock charts and other short-term "tools." The key is not to concern yourself with charts and other things that don't address the *actual value* of a business.

You will resist the tempting enticements of these things because you will be the one to proclaim (or at least realize) that the emperor of Wall Street does not wear any clothes. You will avoid high-tech businesses with uncertain futures and seek out low-tech businesses—franchise-like businesses with big moats around them that consistently generate strong earnings and cash flows without big capital investments. These are the businesses that will be around a decade from now.

You will cultivate the habit of doing a lot of the *right* type of reading, such as the *Wall Street Journal*, and keeping abreast of business events. You will accumulate facts that will form the basis of independent thinking, secure in the knowledge that facts and reasoning—rather than the opinions of others—will determine if you are right or wrong.

You will not mindlessly imitate others. You will develop good habits to help you use all your horsepower. It is these sound principles that explain Warren Buffett's success—and hopefully will explain yours.

To become a sound investor, develop sound investing habits. The investment habits of Warren Buffett provide a detailed roadmap for other investors to follow that will increase their chances of success. Pay attention to the principles and habits of Buffett and you will become a better investor.

Always fight the noise to get the real story. The "real story" of stocks is in the fundamentals. It's not in charts or forecasts or found emanating from the mouths of "talking heads" on the business channels. It's earnings, competitive advantage, enduring brands, and so on.

Always practice continuous improvement. The key to investing is to get better at it with time. Learn from other people's mistakes as well as your own. Write down the things you do right as well as the things you do wrong. Work toward doing more of the former and less of the latter.

It's less about solving difficult business problems, says Warren Buffett, and more about avoiding them. It's about finding and stepping over "one-foot hurdles" rather than developing the extraordinary skills needed to clear seven-foot hurdles.

Further Reading

Warren Buffett's annual reports on BerkshireHathaway .com have been a treasure trove of information for this book and are a must-read. The following books are tremendous sources of information on Buffett and Berkshire Hathaway: *The Making of an American Capitalist* by Roger Lowenstein and *Of Permanent Value* by Andrew Kilpatrick.

✔   ✔   ✔

Sanjeer Parsad is also an excellent source of information on Warren Buffett. To find out more you can go to the Web site: groups.msn.com/BerkshireHathawayShareholders.

Other Titles in the McGraw-Hill Professional Education Series

The Welch Way: 24 Lessons from the World's Greatest CEO
by Jeffrey A. Krames (0-07-138750-1)

The Powell Principles: 24 Lessons from Colin Powell, the Legendary Leader
by Oren Harari (0-07-141109-7)

How to Motivate Every Employee: 24 Proven Tactics to Spark Productivity in the Workplace
by Anne Bruce (0-07-141333-2)

The New Manager's Handbook: 24 Lessons for Mastering Your New Role
by Morey Stettner (0-07-141334-0)

The Handbook for Leaders: 24 Lessons for Extraordinary Leadership
by John H. Zenger and Joseph Folkman (0-07-143532-8)

About the Author

James Pardoe is the principal attorney with Pardoe & Associates and one of today's most knowledgeable followers of Warren Buffett. He received his JD from Pepperdine University.